let go

Live Free of the Burdens All Women Know

Sheila Walsh

THOMAS NELSON
Since 1798

NASHVILLE DALLAS MEXICO CITY RIO DE JANEIRO

Published in Nashville, Tennessee. Thomas Nelson is a registered trademark of Thomas Nelson, Inc.

Thomas Nelson, Inc. titles may be purchased in bulk for educational, business, fund-raising, or sales promotional use. For information, please e-mail SpecialMarkets@ThomasNelson.com.

ISBN 978-1-4002-0302-4 (trade paper)

The Library of Congress has cataloged the hardcover edition as follows:

Walsh, Sheila, 1956–
Let go : live free of the burdens all women know / Sheila Walsh.
p. cm.
Includes bibliographical references.
ISBN 978-0-8499-0135-5
1. Christian women—Religious life. 2. Providence and government of God—Christianity. 3. Trust in God. I. Title.
BV4527.W355 2008
248.8'43—dc22 2008044837

Printed in the United States of America

11 12 13 14 15 RRD 10 9 8 7 6 5 4 3 2 1

CONTENTS

INTRODUCTION

God's rescue plan—to be delivered, you have to let go

One Sunday morning, as I was getting ready for church, I felt discouraged and bone weary. Belle, our three-year-old bichon frise, looked up at me with heartfelt empathy, as if to say, "If you're going down, I'm coming with you." That's how I felt that morning. Many things in my life were going very well, but there were a few areas where I felt very hopeless.

As I looked at my reflection in the mirror, I heard God speak four words to me:

I will deliver you!

I didn't hear an audible voice, but in my spirit God's voice was unmistakable. I was startled by the clarity of the message.

This is not a common occurrence for me. I often hear God speak through the Bible, through my pastor or friends, or through the beauty of nature. But very rarely have I heard his voice so commanding, clear, and deeply personal: *I will deliver you!*

It seemed as if my bathroom floor had become holy ground. I

knew deep down exactly what situation God was assuring me that he would deliver me from. To pretend any longer that the issue that had been weighing on my heart and soul like a frozen winter lake was under control was stretching even Belle's blind devotion, never mind the almighty, all-knowing God of the universe.

I thought, *How will God deliver me from this?* My question revealed a lot about my attitude to being rescued. I am more comfortable with a straightforward scenario—I have a problem, God rescues me, and we all move on with life. But God wants much more for us. God wants to extend us a freedom that goes far beyond a one-time intervention; he wants us to experience a lifestyle of liberty.

My question was answered quickly and clearly, as God's words came ringing back to me: *I will deliver you!*

As I heard God's strong and loving voice again, I knew that the "how" had nothing to do with me. Not only that, but the "how" was ridiculous in light of the "who."

All God was asking me to do was receive his promise and trust him. Nothing more.

I prayed a very simple prayer in response: "Father, thank you. I believe you, I trust you, and I will try to rest in your promise. I have no idea what my deliverance will look like or when it will come, but you do and that's all I need to know. Please give me your grace on the days when I will find it hard to trust and look for more. Help me to let go when I want to try to fix things that only you can fix."

what does it mean to be delivered?

That morning at church, "coincidentally," our pastor taught from the apostle Paul's letter to the church in Philippi:

> I want you to know, brethren, that the things which happened to me have actually turned out for the furtherance of the gospel, so that it has become evident to the whole palace guard, and to all the rest, that my chains are in Christ. . . . and in this I rejoice, yes, and will rejoice. For I know that this will turn out for my deliverance through your prayer and the supply of the Spirit of Jesus Christ. (Philippians 1:12–13, 18–19)

As I reflected on that passage during the next few days, my mind was flooded with questions:

- How did Paul know his present circumstances would work out for his deliverance?
- What does it mean to be delivered?
- Does deliverance always involve a change of circumstances, or do the circumstances sometimes remain the same while God changes us?
- Is there a biblical time frame for how and when deliverance takes place?
- Does God always deliver his children? If not, why not?
- Does every believer need to be delivered?

I knew that I needed answers—and that I shouldn't give up until I had more peace about the issue. So I began this quest to study and understand what it means as a believer to be *delivered*.

How about you? Have you ever wondered what it means to be delivered? To feel delivered? God's declaration that he would deliver me implied many things that caused me to stop and think. If he would deliver me, then I needed to let go of the pieces of the puzzle I couldn't make fit, no matter how hard I tried. That was a struggle for me because each piece was precious, and I felt as if I should be able to make them fit. I sensed, though, that God was offering much more than a quick-fix or rescue; he was offering me a whole new way to live. I wasn't sure if I was ready or even had the stamina for the journey that might lie ahead. Even so, the choices were painfully clear. I could continue to struggle all alone, pushing myself through one more day, or I could take God at his word—and let go.

start with grace

I don't know what made you pick up this book. You may be in financial trouble, in a bad marriage or a difficult relationship, shackled by the pain of your past, or simply want to live in all the fullness that Christ offers. Whatever the case, I imagine that somewhere deep inside you, you long to be delivered. Set free. And so I welcome you to this book. I hope and pray it will be a blessing to you. And I want you to know I will be beside you on this journey.

I also want you to know that I value your time and energy. Very few women have spare time to sit around and think, *Well, what can I do now?* Because of that awareness, I have carefully chosen the biblical insights and personal stories in this book to make a difference in your life and in your walk with Christ.

We will examine many of the issues women often struggle with—but before we do, I believe that the perfect place to begin is with grace. If, like me, you have exhausted your own resources, you are in the perfect place to receive God's grace. Where law imprisons, grace liberates. If you are being beaten up internally or externally by the merciless taskmaster of the law, there is fresh grace available just for you.

Perhaps you are weighed down by events in your past. My heart aches as I think of the time that we as daughters of Eve have lost living in regret. Christ died to put us right with God. He paid for the crushing debt that caused a breach in our relationship with our Father, yet so often we spend our lives in debtors' court as if the bill was still to be paid. Dear sister, you are free—you just have to let go.

What if you are imprisoned by unforgiveness? We live on a fallen planet where terrible injustices rain down on us, often when we are least prepared. When the wound comes from the hand of someone we trusted, the pain and resulting anger can be crippling. I have discovered that one of the most powerful spiritual weapons God has tucked into our arsenal is the gift of forgiveness. Revenge makes us feel powerful, but it handicaps us. It is one of the most difficult things to let go of. Perhaps that is why when we learn by God's grace to let go of revenge and to embrace forgiveness, the freedom that results is outrageous.

Are you plagued by recurring habits that seem to keep you from being the woman you want to be? Have you given your weaknesses the food they most desire, secrecy? There are freedom and deliverance from every act or behavior you hide and grace to love and accept yourself in the process.

Secrecy's cellmate is shame. Shame tells you that you don't belong, that you are hopelessly flawed, not worth loving or saving. Christ's death on the cross for you is a deafening cry to the contrary. In this book, we will look at the journey of the Lamb of God, who became your shame so that you can become God's beloved daughter.

Do you ever find yourself questioning the purpose of your life? Does it matter that you work so hard at taking care of your family? Does anyone really care that you conduct all your business with integrity and honor? As you wait in line to wash your hands in the ladies' restroom on Sunday morning, do the women gossiping in front of you know or care that you were the one who put fresh soap in the dispensers and fresh flowers on the counter? In a culture that worships charisma over character, I want to show you that your life matters to God. It's as if we have been let in on a divine joke where what seems to matter doesn't matter at all, and things our culture brushes under the carpet as insignificant service will one day be revealed to be pure gold when God pulls back the carpet's edge.

What about fear? Do you find yourself looking to the future with dread, wondering how your life will unfold? Are you held back from taking godly risks because of the what-ifs? In a world where there was no God, fear would not only be appropriate; it would be inevitable. That is not your birthright. As a daughter of the King, you are living out the pages of a love story. Don't confuse this love story with the stuff of daytime dramas and Hollywood hype. This love story is sealed with the precious blood of Christ. You are his, and no one can snatch you out of his hand.

Are you lonely? Many of us live busy, lonely lives. We can be surrounded by people, even family, and still feel isolated and alone. It's risky to be known. What if in a moment of finally stepping out of our cocoon, ready to spread our wings and fly, someone laughs at us—or worse still, simply turns her back and continues with her conversation? When a child is born and the very first face she focuses her eyes on is the face of her adoring mother, part of the rip of Eden is healed. When that love and acceptance are further strengthened through the years by her father, and by family and friends, it will be hard to convince this little one that she is not worth loving. The trouble with the human experience of many is that the love they needed and craved as a child was withheld, and the tear of separation that began in Eden has gotten bigger. One of the greatest spiritual gifts of rebirth when we give our lives to Christ is that we have fresh eyes to look into and see how much we are treasured. You have a Father who adores you, who delights in your laugh, who celebrates your gifts, and who catches every tear that falls from your eyes. His love will give you the courage to leave the cocoon behind and fly.

Perhaps you begin this journey as I did, experiencing a level of hopelessness. As you look at your circumstances, you despair of anything ever changing. It's not that you doubt that God is in control, but you live in a world where the decisions of others often affect your life. Can God deliver you even before your circumstances change? I believe that he can. I have and am experiencing that he can. So these are the issues we will look at together. We will look at our own stories and the stories of others, and we will dig deep into the Word of God.

Our Lord and Savior Jesus Christ wants to deliver you into the grace and peace that are your birthright as his child. Jesus left all the glory that was his and embraced all the brokenness and sin that is ours so that we can be free—truly free.

As we begin our journey together in this book, this is my prayer for you:

> Dear Father,
>
> As we stand at the gateway of this book, we ask that by your grace, you will anoint our ears so that we can hear. Anoint our eyes so that we can see. Anoint our hearts and give to us the will to follow you.
>
> In Jesus' name, amen.

ONE

fresh-baked grace for the spiritually hungry

Here it is in a nutshell: Just as one person did it wrong and got us in all this trouble with sin and death, another person did it right and got us out of it. But more than just getting us out of trouble, he got us into life! One man said no to God and put many people in the wrong; one man said yes to God and put many in the right. All that passing laws against sin did was produce more lawbreakers. But sin didn't, and doesn't, have a chance in competition with the aggressive forgiveness we call *grace.* When it's sin versus grace, grace wins hands down.

—Romans 5:18–20 msg

A state of mind that sees God in *everything* is evidence of growth in grace and a thankful heart.

—Charles G. Finney

Grace binds you with far stronger cords than the cords of duty or obligation can bind you. Grace is free, but when once you take it, you are bound forever to the Giver and bound to catch the spirit of the Giver. Like produces like. Grace makes you gracious, the Giver makes you give.

—E. Stanley Jones

let go

So we're not giving up. How could we! Even though on the outside it often looks like things are falling apart on us, on the inside, where God is making new life, not a day goes by without his unfolding grace.

—2 Corinthians 4:16 msg

That is the mystery of grace: it never comes too late.

—François Mauriac

She never wanted her children to worry, but the loss of her husband had been devastating. Some days, the only thing that helped her get out of bed in the morning was knowing that she had three hungry mouths expecting to "Snap, Crackle, and Pop."

Without her husband's salary, the family struggled, especially when it came time to buy clothing. The girls were easier to keep well dressed—through the kindness of friends in her small church who had daughters just a little older than her girls, there was a steady supply of skirts and sweaters.

It was harder with her son. He had one friend in the church, but he was the same age and size, so when pants and shirts were too small for the friend, they were too small for her boy too. And he was growing so fast, it was clear his school pants were far too short.

She didn't have any extra money that month to purchase new pants, so she decided to ask God for help.

Although she didn't want the children to worry, she did want them to know they were being watched over by a very practical, loving Father who understood their needs and was willing and able to meet them. After supper that night, she told them what was going on.

"Your brother needs new pants and I don't have enough money to buy them, so we're going to ask God to provide them," she said.

The younger daughter was skeptical. "Does God keep extra pants in heaven? I didn't think angels wore pants," she said.

"That will not be a problem to God," the mother said with a smile. "If God can make a planet out of nothing, he can certainly find some pants for your brother."

So they joined hands, and she prayed, "Father God, thank you for taking care of us. Thank you that you know what we need even before we ask. But you have invited us to ask in Jesus' name. You know that we have a need for pants, so I ask you to provide those and thank you in advance for your loving provision."

"What now?" the younger girl inquired. "Will an angel ring the doorbell or will the pants come in the mail?"

"Let's just wait and see!" the mother said with a conspiratorial wink.

The following evening, the mother's friend dropped by for a cup of tea. When she left, she gave her a package. "I bought these for Tom, but he seems to have grown several inches overnight! These are far too short. Could your son wear them?"

Inside the mother found three pairs of brand-new pants that were just perfect for her son. She was deeply grateful . . . but you could have knocked the younger daughter over with a feather.

seeing God in everything

Charles Finney once said, "A state of mind that sees God in *everything* is evidence of growth in grace and a thankful heart."[1] That statement was a timely challenge for me. Do you ever read something like that and recognize the truth in the words, yet you struggle with what "seeing God in everything" looks like in real, day-to-day life?

Take your life at this moment and run it through that grid. Is it hard to see the hand of God in *everything* that is happening right now? What are you dealing with right now that you don't remember signing up for?

I think of one of my friends whose daughter is sick. She and her husband are waiting for test results. I think of a school friend of Barry's whose young son has been very ill and has gone through so many painful procedures—and he is not out of the woods yet. I think of a female soldier in Iraq who wrote to say that she listens to audiotapes from our Women of Faith conferences, and at times they are the only thing that keep her sane when she sees friends' lives lost in the war.

All these and other harsh intruders in life often make it hard to recognize the fact that our God is always present. But some of the greatest surprises to me on this spiritual journey are those moments when it becomes clear God has been faithfully cultivating my heart—those times when things don't go as planned, and I *do* see God is in control. They don't have to be extreme situations like I described above. Often it's in the little things we see God's work. That is grace, and that is a gift.

the best-laid plans of mice and men

I didn't realize at the time I read Charles Finney's statement and wrote it in my notebook that God had tucked this little phrase into my pocket for a day like yesterday. As I reflect on the events of yesterday, I'm not sure whether to laugh or cry. Either way, I am a recipient of grace. Let me give you a little background.

In January 2008, Barry and I decided that since we hadn't had a real vacation in five years, our family would travel somewhere fun for spring break. Barry did some research and found a great deal at a hotel in Cancún, Mexico. Since we live in Texas and Cancún is only a two-hour flight for us, it seemed ideal.

A few days before we left, I pulled together everything I thought we'd need. I looked at our three passports and noticed Christian's had expired. Barry called the airline and was told that all we needed for Christian was his birth certificate.

The big day arrived and we got to the airport in lots of time to catch our morning flight. We presented our two passports and Christian's birth certificate at the desk.

The agent asked, "Where's the third passport?"

"We don't have one," Barry said, "but we do have his birth certificate."

"You can't fly without a passport," she said.

"But we called and talked to one of your agents," Barry replied, his bubble of hope beginning to vaporize.

"You can't travel out of the country without a passport—everyone knows that!" she said, looking at us as if we had just crawled out from underneath a haystack.

"That's why we called, ma'am," Barry bravely continued.

"Not my problem," she said. "Next in line!"

By this point Christian was in tears. I felt so bad for him. He had been very excited about our vacation, and now we were stuck at the airport with a plethora of luggage and nowhere to go, and the friend who dropped us off had left.

"I'm so sorry, Christian," I said. "We'll try to work something out."

Christian and I dragged our bags over to a seating area while Barry remained at the counter, trying to fix the problem. Thirty minutes later, we called for a cab. As soon as we arrived back home, we immediately got online to see what could be done. We discovered that if we could get to Houston, Texas, the passport office there could issue Christian a passport when it opened the following morning and we should have it the same day. We drove back to the airport and got on a flight to Houston.

"We'll find a hotel close to the passport office or the airport when we get there," Barry said.

Oh, really?

When we arrived in Houston, we called every hotel we could think of; but they were all full. We got down to the Motel 6, the Motel 5, and the Motel 2½, but there was no room in the inn. Apparently there was a convention of helicopter pilots in town—who knew there were so many! Finally, as we were about to start looking for a stable and manger, we found a hotel with one room left. By this point, we were all very hungry and tired.

"Mom, do you think I could have a steak?" Christian asked. "I'm starving."

"It's your vacation, babe," I said. "Let's see what the hotel has to offer."

Well, that would be . . . nothing. They told us their restaurant was closed, but they would be happy to drive us to one. We told the desk clerk we wanted a steak place, but not anything too formal since we looked a bit bedraggled by this point. She told us about a great restaurant with a new chef who used to work at the Bellagio hotel in Las Vegas. Frankly I didn't care if he'd worked at a Denny's in Darfur; we just needed to eat. The hotel van dropped us off outside a steakhouse and said they would pick us up in an hour. Perfect!

We sat down at our table, and I picked up my menu. I suddenly became painfully aware that Christian was kicking me in the ankle.

"What are you doing, babe?" I asked.

"Mom, that woman is naked!" he whispered.

I looked up and for the first time became aware of the fact that the walls were covered in red velvet and festooned with black-and-white pictures of women with no tops on!

"Barry! Look at the walls!" I said, but he already was.

"Good grief, what is this place?" I whispered. I looked at my menu. It was called The Strip Place. I had naively thought that applied to the strip steak—but apparently not.

Christian went into dramatic mode. "My eyes, my eyes; my beautiful, innocent eyes!"

I said to him, "Just keep your eyes down. Look at your napkin."

When he exploded with laughter, I realized that the same people who'd done the walls had obviously designed the napkins too.

In my evangelical panic, I thought, *Let's sing a hymn; we'll sing a hymn!* What came to mind was one of my grandmother's favorites, "Rock of Ages." Verse two seemed beyond poignant:

Nothing in my hands I bring,
Simply to thy cross I cling.
Naked *come to thee for dress . . .*

I added my own earnest plea to that of Augustus M. Toplady:

Lord, please get me out of this mess;
Good grief, look at the size of that woman's chest!

We were stuck. We were hungry, we had no transport, and we were surrounded by pictures of women showing us how good God had been to them.

"Okay, Christian, here's the deal," I said. "I know we don't normally let you watch mp3 movies in restaurants, but this is what I would describe as . . . unusual circumstances. So put on *Sponge Bob SquarePants*, and don't look up until I am approaching your mouth with a forkful of something."

Well, we made it through dinner and got back to our hotel. After we had our *extended* devotions and prayed together, Christian asked me, "Do you think that made God angry?"

"Do you mean angry that we stayed?" I asked.

"I don't know, Mom—just the whole thing," he said.

"I don't think God was cross with us at all," I told him. "I think it made him sad that those ladies felt they had to take off their clothes. I know he loves them and wants the best for them."

"Do you think he loves them as much as he loves you?" he asked.

"Every bit as much," I said.

"Even though they're doing something he wouldn't want them to?" he asked.

"Christian, God's love for us is not based on our behavior," I assured him. "It's based on his heart and his character. That's grace."

grace in all things

I am aware that this silly inconvenience doesn't hold a candle to the life-and-death situations I described earlier. But that's actually my point. As a believer of forty years (I gave my life to Christ when I was eleven), when I am faced with life's crises, I usually know enough to turn to God for strength, grace, and guidance. It's the small stuff that gets me. It's the moments when my plans are messed up, and it feels like no one really cares one way or another. Those are the times I must learn the lesson over again—to trust God. It's hard for me, because it means I have to let go of my agenda.

As Christian and I sat there in the airport in Dallas surrounded by our bags and disappointment, it was a moment of true humanity and grace to let our heads touch as we asked God to help us through. We didn't have to be strong. We didn't have to do it on our own. We didn't need to follow any rules or live up to any expectations. We just had to be honest and real.

We finally made it to Cancún two days late. But we were there. The three of us sat on the beach, side by side, as the sun was setting. Christian said, "Well, it sure took a while to get here, and I saw things no grandson of a Baptist should ever see, but God was with us every step."

For me, that is the miracle of grace. Not that we finally made it to our vacation, but that God was with us every step—and an eleven-year-old boy knew it, even when our plans seemed to fall apart.

As I look back over my life, I can think of many times when this kind of situation happened and my response was very different. I know now that God's grace was right there every single time, but sometimes I didn't reach out and receive it. To have my hands free to receive grace, I have to be willing to let go of whatever I am clinging to.

Think about your own journey. Can you see in your own life how you are growing in grace, not just in the big moments but all those little moments that can rob us of peace and joy?

that's not fair!

As I have watched my son grow in his understanding of grace, the greatest obstacle for him has been the way he often connects God's favor to his behavior. Christian thinks when we do good things God applauds our righteous behavior, and when we slip and fall he frowns on us. (Do you know how hard it is for me as a mother not to let that belief sit there for a few more years, until he's, say, thirty?) I have to tell him again and again God is not a Scout leader or an etiquette coach. His love is lavish and without repentance.

I think this is one of the hardest doctrines to wrap our hearts and minds around. There is something in us that wants to feel we have contributed in some way to whatever we receive. With the grace of God, we contribute nothing. That's hard for us to swallow. We know we don't bring as much as God does to the table, but we want to feel as if we've done our bit for the team! Not only that, but God's grace is fresh every single day, which means you don't have to rely on what was available yesterday. In fact, yesterday's grace is stale. Yesterday's grace was baked fresh by God for the events of yesterday, but today there is a whole new supply for every single thing you will walk through today.

Christian is not a big breakfast eater. He often runs out to shoot hoops with his friends on a summer morning with nothing more than the aftertaste of toothpaste in his system. Then he'll come dragging in and say, "Mom, I'm starving!"

Do you ever find yourself spiritually starving halfway through your day? Fresh grace is available from the moment you open your eyes until you crawl back under the covers at night.

When we are satiated with God's grace, it is much easier to extend grace to others; but when we are on starvation rations ourselves, we have little to spare.

There is also something in us that finds it hard to see that same lavish grace extended to those who seem particularly undeserving. Perhaps no parable illustrates that more clearly than one found in Matthew's gospel. Jesus told the story of a vineyard owner who hired his first workers of the day at 6 a.m. and agreed on a wage of one dollar. He hired more field hands at 9 a.m., noon, 3 p.m., and 5 p.m.

When it came time to pay the day's wages, he told the foreman to begin with those who had worked only the last hour. When the workers who had sweated in the field all day realized that the tail-end stragglers were receiving one dollar, they were encouraged for a moment, assuming their own paycheck had been bumped up exponentially. Not so. They were given the same dollar as the rest. The workers who had worked all day were furious, and they appointed the loudest mouth in the group to complain to the manager. But the manager wouldn't entertain their argument.

> He replied to the one speaking for the rest, "Friend, I haven't been unfair. We agreed on the wage of a dollar, didn't we? So take it and go. I decided to give to the one who came last the same as you. Can't I do what I want with my own money? Are you going to get stingy because I am generous?" Here it is again, the Great Reversal: many of the first ending up last, and the last first. (Matthew 20:13–16 MSG)

The kingdom of God has nothing to do with our scales of justice. From our perspective, it's easy to pick out the good guys and the bad guys; but God says there is no such thing as a good guy. We are all sinners standing in need of the grace of God: "Scripture leaves no doubt about it: There's nobody living right, not even one, nobody who knows the score, nobody alert for God" (Romans 3:9–10 MSG).

If you're like me, you've thought, *Well, sure, I understand that we're all sinners in a broad sense, Lord, but there are some of us who mess up a lot less than others. You can't tell me that doesn't count for something.*

It is so tempting to categorize sin, to see others as less deserving of God's grace than we are. The clarion call of a grace-filled life is that we are required to lay down our internal scales of justice, not only as we see ourselves but also as we see and judge others. In terms of our salvation and God's love for us, our list of what we view as our good behavior counts for nothing.

the promise of grace

We've looked at the problem of legalism, so now it's time to embrace the promise of grace. It's hard to extend to others what you have not allowed yourself to be blessed by, but the truth remains:

- As you are, right at this moment, God loves you.
- He knows all that is true about you, and he loves you.
- Even when you can't forgive yourself, he forgives you.
- There is nothing you can do to make him love you more.
- There is nothing you can do to make him love you less.

This is the grace of God.

Take a few moments and be quiet with these truths. How do they sit with you? Are they hard to believe? Perhaps as we look at our past and bring it to the foot of the cross, it will help us receive the grace of God. Remember, as Martin Luther said, "A man must completely despair of himself in order to become fit to obtain the grace of Christ."[2]

deliverance discovered

1. Do you believe—not just in your head, but deep in your soul—that God loves you as you are right now? Explain.
2. Do you think there is anything you could do to make God love or approve of you more? Explain.
3. Who in your circle do you find it the most difficult to extend grace to?
4. Why do you think that is?

a prayer of deliverance

Father God,

Thank you for the grace you offer me right at this moment. Deliver me from self-doubt and fear.

Help me to feast on your glorious gift of fresh-baked grace every morning. Thank you that your love and grace invite us all to the feast. May I share this feast with someone else today.

For Jesus' sake, amen.

TWO

this dead religion is past its sell-by date

This only I want to learn from you: Did you receive the Spirit by the works of the law, or by the hearing of faith? Are you so foolish? Having begun in the Spirit, are you now being made perfect by the flesh? Have you suffered so many things in vain—if indeed it was in vain?

—Galatians 3:2–4

Some of the most virtuous men in the world are also the bitterest and most unhappy because they have unconsciously come to believe that all their happiness depends on their being more virtuous than other men.

—Thomas Merton

Let your religion be less of a theory and more of a love affair.

—G. K. Chesterton

When Christ died he took that entire rule-dominated way of life down with him and left it in the tomb, leaving you free to "marry" a resurrection life and bear "offspring" of faith for God.

—Romans 7:4 msg

Rules blunt the appetite for Christ. Joy intrigues.

—Calvin Miller

She was sure her bag was heavier today than it was yesterday. Or perhaps, she reasoned, she was just worn-out from everything going on in her life. She hadn't slept well the previous night and had awakened with such a headache.

She poured coffee into a thermos and headed out the door, catching a glimpse of her pale face in the glass. As she stepped outside, the insistent ringing of the phone dragged her back inside her apartment.

"We missed you last night," a voice said with a definite edge.

"Yes, I'm sorry. I got home late and was so tired, and I hadn't taken the dog for a walk in two days. And I'm not—"

"Oh, we understood," the voice cut in. "It's just so easy to get into bad habits. Remember, the believer who tries to stand alone is easy prey for the enemy."

"Yes, I know, but it's just that—"

"You missed the prayer meeting last week as well. It's not enough to just pop in on Sunday mornings, you know," the voice insisted. "If you want to be part of the body of Christ, you have to show up and do your part."

"I'm actually finding it kind of hard to do my part right now," she said.

"And, quite honestly, we feel that. Well, let's see if you can get a couple of early nights in so that you can be back to your best by Sunday."

"I'll try, it's just that—"

"Good-bye now!"

"It's just that . . . I have chemotherapy on Wednesday nights now . . ."

But the voice was gone.

longing to be heard

We all long to be heard. We want to be seen as we really are, not as we at times appear to be. Like the woman in the story, we wish that life would slow down enough for us to be able to talk about what we're dealing with. I'm sure the person on the phone was well intentioned, but good intentions can often leave us cold and alone. We long to be seen as real people, not just numbers in the church attendance register.

Have you ever wished your friends, those in your small group, or even your spouse could hear behind what you're saying to what's really going on in your heart? Have you thought, *Can't they see it in my eyes? Don't they know I'm sinking fast?*

Unfortunately, we live in a very fast-paced world, and all too often we find ourselves at the end of another day without having connected with anyone in a meaningful way. Why is that? Is it because others don't want to listen to or see our need? Or is it because we're unwilling to reveal that need? Or both?

Most often, I imagine, we don't tell others about our needs because we don't want to be thought less of. Have you ever felt misunderstood or judged by a Christian friend? If so, you know it's one of the most painful hurts the human soul can sustain. Perhaps you once took a risk and told a friend of your struggles—and instead of finding comfort, you experienced condemnation. Perhaps it happened at a time when you were already feeling vulnerable, and your friend's response made the pain all the more intense. Instead of feeling more known, you felt more alone. So you learned to just hold it in.

Human hearts are not rule-shaped, and when others try to squeeze us into their version of acceptability, it always causes wounds. We all long to be known, but because we fear others' reactions we have learned to guard ourselves. It is not always safe to be known.

But what if we're the ones causing the pain? What if we're not the judged but the judgers?

no flowers for my boy

I met her at a women's conference. I had been asked as a speaker to open and close a day filled with seminars and workshops. We bumped into each other in the corridor outside the main hall as we both tried to find our way to a particular room. As we walked together, we talked and discovered we had the most precious thing in common: we are both mothers of a boy. She's further down the road with her son, who is now out of high school. Christian will have turned twelve, God willing, by the time you read this book.

"I wish I had known what I know now when my son was twelve," she said.

"What would you have done differently?" I asked, hoping to pick up a few tips.

"I would have opened my eyes to the truth," she said. "I would have shaken myself out of denial."

This was more than I'd seen coming, so I stopped walking and listened as she told me some of her son's story. It was a sad tale of drug and alcohol addiction. She adopted him when he was just a baby and had no idea he had a strong genetic predisposition to addiction. He gave his life to Christ as a young boy and has prayed over and over to be delivered, but the battle is fierce. He has been in and out of treatment programs, wrestling with the demons that torment him.

I asked her what her greatest challenge or heartache has been, and her answer surprised me: she said it was watching how others in their church treated her son.

"If he had a brain tumor or cancer, they would be over with casseroles and flowers. But there are no flowers for my boy. People don't understand he is sick. They just think he is weak or a bum," she said with tears in her eyes.

All she longed for was companionship and understanding on this terrible path she had to walk. Yet at the time when she needed us—the church—most, she felt our comfort the least.

I have to admit I had never thought of drug addiction or alcoholism that way. It's easy to put these struggles into the category of weakness or sin, but the reality is those whose brains are wired toward addiction go through tremendous pain if they try to break free. Everything within their bodies and brains craves the next hit the way a man lost in the desert craves water. And as if that isn't enough, those who battle addiction often feel the pain and isolation of our judgment.

As I thought over our conversation, I began to wonder how much alienation goes on in Christian circles—how many times Christians try to shove others into their versions of perfection. I was uncomfortably aware that the answer was probably "a lot." It doesn't have to be the extremes of this type of abuse. It can be as simple as ridiculing different forms of worship. It can relate to what kind of school you send your children to or what rating of movie or video game you allow them to play.

It is very easy to judge when others appear to choose an option we don't allow in our home. Let me give you an example I'm not exactly proud of.

a rush to judgment

Barry and I have pretty strict rules for our son, Christian, particularly about the video games he plays on his Xbox. There was a game that was very popular in Christmas 2007, and Christian asked if he could get it. Barry and I did a little research online, and it became clear the game was not suitable for Christian's age.

Each day after that, he came home from school with an ever-lengthening list of boys in his class who were now getting the game. I finally said, "Look, Christian, I don't care if Billy Graham endorses the game and it comes with a free Bible and a John 3:16 tattoo, we are not buying it, babe."

He seemed to get my point and life moved on, but there was a subtle shift inside my heart. I am pretty friendly with the moms of two of the boys on Christian's list, and I found myself setting up a little courtroom in my mind with me as self-appointed judge and jury.

"Now, 'Melissa,' is it true that on December 23, 2007, you did purchase one copy of the game I now hold in my hand as prosecutor's exhibit A?"

"Yes," she whispers.

"Louder, please, so that the whole court may hear."

"Yes," she replies at an acceptable volume.

"And is it also true that this game is rated 'M' for 'Mature Audiences'?"

"Yes."

"Having observed your son at my son's last birthday party, mature is not the first word that would come to mind. I love him dearly, but I seem to remember him hanging over the edge of the ice rink calling out to the ice hockey players, 'We want blood!'"

"Melissa" smiles. A brave or brazen move? I wonder.

"Do you have anything to say in your defense?" I ask, preparing to send my case to the jury.

"Yes. It's not his game."

"But you just admitted purchasing it. Are you going back on your previous, sworn statement?"

"No, I'm not," she says kindly. "We bought the game for his brother, 'Steve.' He's nineteen."

Ouch!

Fortunately this little drama took place only in my mind. But the fact that it took place at all is interesting to me. When did I decide it was up to me to dictate how others should live their lives and what their faith should look like?

Now, you might be gracious enough to come to my defense and support my parenting position, but it's the spirit beneath it I'm interested in here. Clearly, ratings are put in place for very good reasons, and I will do everything I can to protect Christian from the junk this world is siphoning down the throats of our children. But I need to guard my heart against self-righteousness. It is so easy to subtly judge someone and allow that judgment to put a barrier between us. Then if we really want to cap the whole thing off with our version of the Hallelujah Chorus, we'll just offer to pray for them!

"Sic 'em, God!"

This can be a bit of a gray area as a parent. Obviously I don't want Christian spending the night with a friend whose parents are happy to let them watch *Dawn of the Dead*. But there are ways of monitoring that without dismissing the family in the process. How often have you found yourself pulling back just a little from someone when you disapprove of the choice she made?

Jesus told his friends to go out into the world and share the gospel, not their opinions. It's what we do to one another with our words, our tone, and our body language that can make others feel isolated and judged. Have you felt that? Or have you, like me, been the one to dish it out? Did you feel justified in doing so?

the difference between the law and legalism

There have been many wonderful books written on the subject of God's law and grace at war with legalism. Chuck Swindoll's *The Grace Awakening* is one of the best books I have read on the subject, as is Lewis Smedes's *Shame and Grace.*[1] So I won't delve into the nuts and bolts of the dilemma. For our purposes, I want us to look at what legalism does to our freedom in Christ and to our relationships with one another.

As we saw in his letter to the church in Rome, Paul expressed the common cry of every believer who tries to live up to the standards of the law and fails miserably: "What I will to do, that I do not practice; but what I hate, that I do. . . . O wretched man that I am! Who will deliver me from this body of death?" (Romans 7:15, 24). The interesting double standard, though, is that we still try to make others live up to what we cannot. That is legalism, and it is deadly. It is so easy to take the word of the law and miss the heart.

I believe there is a gulf between the law given by God to protect his people and the legalism that has such a death grip on the lives of many believers today. The law comes from the heart of a loving God who wants to protect his people—and is translated on our part into both loving obedience and a desire to encourage and help others. Legalism comes from a cold insistence by those who want to enforce their standards on everyone else.

The first five books of the Old Testament—Genesis, Exodus, Leviticus, Numbers, and Deuteronomy—are known collectively as the Pentateuch, or the books of the Law. As we examine the laws given by God to his people, they reveal much more than rules; they reveal his heart. God prefaced the Ten Commandments by restating his relationship with his children: "I am the Lord your God, who brought you . . . out of the house of bondage." (Exodus 20:2).

In Exodus 20:3–17, God clearly outlined these ten laws:

1. Do not worship any other gods besides me.
2. Do not make idols of any kind.
3. Do not misuse the name of the Lord your God.
4. Remember to observe the Sabbath day by keeping it holy.
5. Honor your father and mother.
6. Do not murder.
7. Do not commit adultery.
8. Do not steal.
9. Do not testify falsely against your neighbor.
10. Do not covet anything your neighbor owns.

When you look at these ten laws again (or for the first time), it seems like they shouldn't have been that difficult to follow. Think about it: Honor God and keep him first. Take a day off. Honor your mom and dad. Don't kill anyone. Don't sleep with anyone else's husband. Don't shoplift. Tell the truth. And if your friend has a nice new Coach purse, be happy for her! God wasn't demanding twenty hours of community service every day or six hours of hymn singing before bedtime. He just wanted a few things that, on first examination, should have come naturally. The tragedy is that the Ten Commandments brought into sharp focus our complete inability to obey God in our own strength.

The people of Israel just couldn't do it. They couldn't obey the law because . . . *they were sinners*. Just like us.

In this day of self-help gurus and feel-good books, it's easy to get away from the truth that we are all sinners. We were born into sin as children of Adam and Eve . . . and our culture does not want to hear about it. Look on the best-seller list and you'll find book after book that encourages us to believe we are the light of the world, we are like gods, and all we have to do is embrace that. That is a demonic lie. Our freedom doesn't come from becoming God but by embracing what God has done for us through his Son, Jesus Christ.

Jesus told us that if we follow him, we won't stumble around in the dark because he will give us his light to lead us (John 8:12). There is a huge gap between *following* the Light of the world and *being* the light of the world. It's not popular to talk about sin, but it's the truth.

When you break down the Ten Commandments, all God was asking us to do was to love him and to love one another. Does that sound familiar? Remember when the scribes and Pharisees in Jesus' day accused him of destroying the law? Take a look at what Jesus said when they tried to trip him up:

> When the Pharisees heard how he had bested the Sadducees, they gathered their forces for an assault. One of their religion scholars spoke for them, posing a question they hoped would show him up: "Teacher, which command in God's Law is the most important?"
>
> Jesus said, "'Love the Lord your God with all your passion and prayer and intelligence.' This is the most important, the first on any list. But there is a second to set alongside it: 'Love others as well as you love yourself.' These two commands are pegs; everything in God's Law and the Prophets hangs from them." (Matthew 22:34–40 MSG)

Jesus' response clarifies the difference between legalism and the law. The Pharisees were legalists, trying to impress God by following the letter of the law. But Jesus' surprising answer was this: God was looking at their hearts, not their rule books.

cast your cares, don't "caste" your sister

Legalism reminds me of the caste system that existed in India for many years and still exists in many areas, although it is technically illegal. (I recently read an article in a British newspaper that said the caste system is reemerging among England's Indian community.) The caste system is a form of social hierarchy, and two thousand years ago it divided Hindus into four main categories: priests, warriors or ruling class, merchants, and unskilled laborers. Below them were the untouchables—people deemed so low they could not even be included in the system.

This might seem extreme to you at first, but I believe such a system exists in many parts of the church. We have those at the top—the pastors or bishops, depending on denomination. We have the wealthy members of the congregation who contribute greatly to the financial health of the church and are treated accordingly. Then we have the majority of the people—those who work hard and do their best to make sure their children don't throw their hymnbooks at the woman in front of them. Then there are those who are dependent on the church for help and support. And below them all are the untouchables—like the struggling drug addict who gets no flowers or casseroles.

I don't know what it is within us that wants to put people in their places. Does it make us feel better about ourselves? There seems to be an innate need to find where we fit in the big picture. But rather than accessing God's criteria of love and grace, we use our own human understanding of worth. I wonder how many wonderful opportunities to encounter Christ in others we have missed because of our blurred vision.

the bottom line

A common thread throughout human history is our inability to live up to God's standards. But another thread can be traced: our desire to squeeze people into a mold of our making—to embrace a dead religion rather than a living truth. Both realities would leave us miserable . . . if it weren't for Christ. Moses gave us the Law from God, but Christ himself brought and embodied grace and truth to deliver us from ourselves and from the judgment of one another: "For the law was given through Moses, but grace and truth came through Jesus Christ" (John 1:17).

In *The Message*, Eugene Peterson translated this verse in this jubilant way: "We all live off his generous bounty, gift after gift after gift. We got the basics from Moses, and then this exuberant giving and receiving, this endless knowing and understanding—all this came through Jesus, the Messiah."

The ground at the foot of the cross is even. There are no podiums for those who feel most worthy. There are no pits for those who feel they don't belong. The only way to break free from this dead, stale religion is with the glorious gift of fresh-baked grace every morning for the rest of our lives!

deliverance discovered

1. Have there been times in your life when you felt judged by others? Explain.
2. How did that make you feel?
3. Can you identify ways that you have judged others?
4. What do you think is the difference between accountability (the law) and legalism?

a prayer of deliverance

Father God,

I come to you in the powerful name of Jesus Christ, my Savior and my Lord. I ask that through your Holy Spirit you show me areas in my life that have been crushed by judgment and condemnation. Help me to bring those wounds into your light to be healed.

If I have been guilty of judging others, please show me and help me to make things right. In any area where I have a heart of stone, please give me a heart of love and grace. May I in Jesus' name let go of the stale bread of religion and instead partake of your fresh-baked grace today.

In Jesus' name, amen.

THREE

living in the past

Forget about what's happened; don't keep going over old history. Be alert, be present. I'm about to do something brand-new. It's bursting out! Don't you see it? There it is! I'm making a road through the desert, rivers in the badlands.

—Isaiah 43:18–19 msg

In Christ we can move out of our past into a meaningful present and a breathtaking future.

—Erwin W. Lutzer

There is no past we can bring back by longing for it. There is only an eternal now that builds and creates out of the past something new and better.

—Johann Wolfgang von Goethe

The purpose of being guilty is to bring us to Jesus. Once we are there, then its purpose is finished. If we continue to make ourselves guilty—to blame ourselves—then that is sin in itself.

—Corrie ten Boom

With the arrival of Jesus, the Messiah, that fateful dilemma is resolved. Those who enter into Christ's being-here-for-us no longer have to live under a continuous, low-lying black cloud. A new power is in operation. The Spirit of life in Christ, like a strong wind, has magnificently cleared the air, freeing you from a fated lifetime of brutal tyranny at the hands of sin and death.

—Romans 8:1–2 MSG

She opened the box that had been delivered that morning and peeled back layer upon layer of soft, pink tissue paper. Nestled inside was the most beautiful dress she had ever seen. She pulled it out and held it up to the sun that was streaming through her bedroom window.

The dress was exquisite. It was white and had satin ribbons around the waist that tied in a bow at the back. She tried it on, and it fit as if it had been tailor made. Not usually given to spontaneity or to dancing, she found herself twirling round and round. The ribbons flew out behind her like flags in a summer breeze.

Suddenly, she caught sight of herself in the mirror. She almost didn't recognize herself: light, free, almost childlike. She stopped immediately and took off the dress. Putting it back in the box, she covered it once more with the tissue paper and placed the box under her bed. She took her old gray dress off the chair, pulled it over her head, and straightened her hair in the mirror.

"There," she said. "That's as it should be."

the problem with the past

One of the greatest challenges to living and loving truly free as the women God sees in us is our very own memory banks. We remember all the poor choices we've made in the past and wonder how our lives would have been if we'd done things differently. We look back at times when we were not as strong or didn't know ourselves as well and chastise ourselves for being . . . human. We still blame ourselves for things that were not our fault. But it's hard to shake things we've believed for many years.

Add to that the internal scales by which we still judge our actions every day, and it's no wonder we live with a heavy spirit. We make mistakes, but it's hard to give grace for them. We are human, but as those who love Christ, we want to "get it right."

We read the words of the apostle Paul, who reminded the believers in Rome that for those who are in Christ, there is no condemnation (Romans 8:1). On our internal scales, two realities battle for position—the grace of God versus our self-knowledge. We know that we can't earn the favor of God, yet we long to. We know that when God forgives our sin, it is removed as far as the east is from the west (Psalm 103:12), yet that very sin seems to forever cloud our view.

Not only that, but in our day-to-day lives we have to deal with criticism and judgment from others. And let's not forget the greatest liar and accuser of all—the enemy of our souls.

a familiar song

Have you ever stopped and listened to the tapes that play in your head? It might shock you to hear what you say to yourself. You probably call yourself names you would never dream of calling anyone else. Last year I saw that although I have changed and grown in so many ways, there is still a little girl inside me who, when she feels stressed and under pressure, resorts to familiar patterns.

My dad died when I was a little girl, but my mom still lives in the same small Scottish town where my brother, sister, and I were raised. Mom used to be quite an adventurer. She loved to travel and has been all over the world with me until recently. Now her health at seventy-seven has made it very hard for her to travel at all. She has severe osteoporosis and several fractures in her back. That plus the usual indignities of getting older keep her pretty close to home. So last Thanksgiving I decided to take a quick trip home to see her. Barry had some commitments, but Christian had a whole week off school, so he and I traveled to see Grandma.

It's an eight-hour flight to London, then a one-hour flight from London to Glasgow, Scotland. When we finally arrived, we were tired but very happy to be there. What I hadn't prepared for was how I would cope with trying to be a daughter and a mother at the same time. Part of my dysfunction from my childhood is a huge sense of responsibility for my mother's happiness. This is not something she placed on me but a burden I picked up for myself. The circumstances of my father's death from the repercussions of a massive brain aneurism left me feeling responsible. If you know any of my story you know he and I had a showdown when I was four, and the result of his attempted attack on me had him institutionalized. He died shortly after.

As an adult I know none of what took place was my fault, but as a child I carried tremendous guilt for the past. I saw what I interpreted to be my mother's loneliness and our financial struggle as my fault. When I reached adulthood, I finally received healing in many areas. I have talked with my mom about my feelings, and she has made it crystal clear that nothing that happened was my fault.

So why does some of that stuff still linger?

I rented a car so I could take Mom to some of her favorite spots and find something Christian would enjoy too. The next few days were like a three-ring mind circus for me!

I had told Christian that Grandma's hearing is not what it used to be, so he would need to remember that and make adjustments. He promised to do his best. We did pretty well until the third day of our trip. It was a lovely morning, so we decided to drive down the coast. Mom was in the front of the car and Christian in the back. He had never seen so many fields of pure white sheep and kept pointing them out to me with loud exclamations. Mom couldn't hear him, so she was telling me about all her friends and people I knew from my childhood. Christian was too excited to notice Grandma was also speaking, so he just kept going. I had two of the most important people in my life talking to me at the same time as I tried like a manic nodding dog to listen to both conversations. After lunch at a local farm, Mom said she needed a new battery for her hearing aid, which she could get at the local hospital. I drove her to the front door and dropped her off as I went to park.

I had never been to that hospital, since it was built after I left, but when I went to park I suddenly realized where I was. As I pulled into a spot, I saw that I was facing the old psychiatric hospital where my father died. I looked up at the windows of that bleak place, and something inside me came undone. It was all suddenly too much.

This hospital had been the place of nightmares to me as a child. As I sat there, images from my past seemed to replay inside my head, and I saw how I have always dealt with the pain of the past—by trying to bury the pain beneath a mountain of "stuff," whether it was food or new clothes or going to see three movies in one day. Anything to keep the wounds anesthetized.

As a teenager and into my twenties and early thirties, whenever I felt the familiar sadness creep over me, I stuffed myself with every kind of food I could find. I ate cakes and cookies and candy until I could hardly walk. I didn't even stop to enjoy it; I just shoveled it down.

Then the tape started playing.

- "You idiot, why did you do that?"
- "You should know better!"
- "Just look at yourself."
- "You always do this—what is wrong with you?"

I would never dream of talking to anyone else like that, but I beat myself up for quite some time.

old habits

Have you ever been there? It might not be over a food issue. It could be anything—whatever has the power to shame you. In those situations, the cold hand of the past loves to strangle the love and peace of Christ right out of you. We so easily allow the winter of regret to eradicate the joy of spring and all things new. It's a mental battle that is as powerful as any fought in trenches or in tanks.

What do you do in those moments of negativity? Do you give in to the past, or do you use the past to understand your future in Christ? I hope it's the latter, as hard as that may be sometimes. Dwelling on the past does nothing, but learning from it and then letting it go does. Alice Miller, psychologist and sociologist, said it well: "Experience has taught us that we have only one enduring weapon in our struggle against mental illness: the emotional discovery and emotional acceptance of the truth in the individual and unique history of our childhood."[1]

Not only by the grace of God can we accept what is true about our past, but in Christ our very wounds and scars can be redeemed. Pain is hard; there's no doubt. But pain reminds us why Christ died. It reminds us to bring our wounds to the wounded Healer so he can make us better. In turn, we can comfort others as we have been comforted and look to a future free from hurt. We are not asked to pretend our wounds don't exist, but to let go and stop holding on to them so tightly.

In his book *The Truths We Must Believe,* Dr. Chris Thurman wrote about an intriguing statement: "What should have happened did." Dr. Thurman explained that he got the quote from Paul "Bear" Bryant, former head coach at the University of Alabama. When asked, after a loss against a team they were expected to beat, how he felt about losing the game, Coach Bryant said, "What should have happened did."

On first read, I found myself bristling against this idea . . . until I began to really chew on it.

Think about it. We use the word *should* an awful lot. "I shouldn't have been late." "She should have known better." "The Cowboys shouldn't have lost that game." It's like a cane we bring down on our souls or the souls of others.

But "should" was something we can't control. It is the past, not the future. So why do we spend all our time beating ourselves up for something we can't get back?

Because we're human, that's why.

Coach Bryant was right. If we believe that God controls our course in life, with our best intentions at heart, then "What should have happened did." How freeing!

The truth is that whatever happened in a particular moment of our lives, that's where we were at that moment. We acted on the understanding we had then. In God's sovereignty he brought us from where we were, to where we are right at this moment. We were never alone, never abandoned.

God had quite a surprise for me as I revisited the place where my father died. He brought me full circle so I was no longer a five-year-old girl haunted by a nightmare but a fifty-one-year-old woman comforted by the God of all hope who holds our past, our present, and our future in his hands.

look to the future!

When I look back at the guilt that made me stuff myself silly and pack on the pounds for many years, it's all very well for me to say, "I shouldn't have done that." But the truth is I did. Accepting what *is* enables us to embrace a different future. I can say, "I should be thinner," but the truth is, if I keep shoveling food in my mouth, I should look like I did. Christian could say, "I should have done better on that test," but the truth remains that if you don't study for a test, the result will reflect that.

What should have happened did.

Your pain might be much more acute than the scenarios I describe. Perhaps your father sexually abused you. Perhaps your husband is an alcoholic and came home drunk again last night. Perhaps you're dealing with some serious issues with a child or other family member. You would be justified in asking, "How can you say what should have happened did?"

My answer would simply be that being set free from the past means accepting what is true, not what we wish was true. If you had a father who was sick enough to hurt you, that's who he is. To say it shouldn't have happened is to say that you wish he were a different person. But he was not. And you can't change that reality.

Rather than sink under the devastation of what happened, we add a new truth about what should have happened. We say, "God, you should have been there!" God answers, *My beloved child, I was there. I held you although you could not see my arms. I caught each tear that fell. You were never alone.*

David expressed this truth exquisitely in Psalm 139:

Is there anyplace I can go to avoid your Spirit? to be out of your
sight?
If I climb to the sky, you're there! If I go underground, you're there!
If I flew on morning's wings to the far western horizon,
You'd find me in a minute—you're already there waiting!
Then I said to myself, "Oh, he even sees me in the dark!
At night I'm immersed in the light!"
It's a fact: darkness isn't dark to you;
night and day, darkness and light, they're all the same to you.
(vv. 7–12 MSG)

Please understand: I'm not trying to belittle your situation! What you long for is exactly what each of us longs for in one way or another. But sometimes we have to make peace with what was or is to be able to let go and move on. So many of us put ourselves in situations to be hurt over and over by the same person because we know things *should* be different. We cling to our dreams of what we wish the past could have been and set ourselves up to be hurt again and again. If this is you, I encourage you to let go of that past—your "what should have been"—and embrace your "what is" and your "what can be." Truth is powerful. At times it is heartbreaking, but ultimately, it will deliver you.

Even as we deal with the painful habits of our past, it is important to remember that we have an enemy whose sole focus is to destroy what God loves. And that is you! He is a liar and will drag trash onto the front doorstep of your life every day if you let him. You must remain vigilant against that. As Peter wrote in his first letter: "Stay alert. The Devil is poised to pounce, and would like nothing better than to catch you napping. Keep your guard up" (5:8 MSG).

The devil is a thief who would love to rob you of your identity in Christ. Don't let him. Jesus came to give you life—real life.

Because of Christ, we don't have to live in the past; we can be present today and tomorrow to live a life that is better than one we could have dreamed for ourselves (John 10:10).

Remember that even with the devil "what should happen will." He is a defeated enemy who knows that his days are numbered:

> Then I heard a strong voice out of Heaven saying,
>
> "Salvation and power are established! Kingdom of our God, authority of his Messiah! The Accuser of our brothers and sisters thrown out, who accused them day and night before God." (Revelation 12:10 MSG)

We can make peace with the truth of the past. We can learn from the past. But Christ calls us to be free to live today and tomorrow with purpose and passion.

deliverance discovered

1. Can you identify the negative things you say to yourself?
2. What are issues from the past that you still deal with today?
3. What should-haves do you beat yourself up with?
4. What lies is the evil one whispering to you about your past?
5. Based on the truth of God's Word, how will you respond to Satan's lies about your past?

a prayer of deliverance

Father God,

Thank you that you sent Jesus to free me from the pain of the past and to give me a future and a hope. By your Spirit, help me to bring all the old negative habits to you and leave them there. Help me to identify the lies of the evil one and reject them in your name. Deliver me from the pain of the past, and redeem my scars for the sake of your kingdom.

In Jesus' name, amen.

FOUR

look at the view ahead!

I'm not saying that I have this all together, that I have it made. But I am well on my way, reaching out for Christ, who has so wondrously reached out for me. Friends, don't get me wrong: By no means do I count myself an expert in all of this, but I've got my eye on the goal, where God is beckoning us onward—to Jesus. I'm off and running, and I'm not turning back.

—Philippians 3:12–14 msg

No man ever sank under the burden of the day. It is when tomorrow's burden is added to the burden of today that the weight is more than a man can bear. Never load yourself so. If you find yourself so loaded, at least remember this: it is your own doing, not God's. He begs you to leave the future to him, and mind the present.

—George MacDonald

This is the true joy in life, the being used for a purpose recognized by yourself as a mighty one; the being thoroughly worn out before you are thrown on the scrap heap; the being a force of nature instead of a feverish, selfish little clod of ailments and grievances complaining that the world did not devote itself to making you happy.

—George Bernard Shaw

Because You have been my help,
  Therefore in the shadow of Your wings I will rejoice.
My soul follows close behind You;
  Your right hand upholds me.

—Psalm 63:7–8

The first step was the most difficult. Everything looked strange and new, and that was enough to make her pause. She knew what was inside the four walls of her cottage. She could move around in the dark; everything was so familiar. But out there . . .

The invitation had come as a surprise. It was so personal. Her name was there, written on the top line so there could be no mistake it was meant for her.

She thought of what others might say if they knew that she had been invited into the wide open. Some would laugh, she was sure. Others would say how ridiculous it was to even imagine she could do such a thing. She looked at her right foot, twisted toward her body as if to say, "Don't go; we can't make it out there."

She took one look back at everything she knew and stepped outside. As the sun kissed her face and the wind caught her hair, she knew at that moment she would never go back again.

the promise of fairy tales

As a child, I watched fairy tales through cynical glasses. The kind of disbelief I felt then should not have come till much later in life. When most little girls watch Disney movies or listen to classic fairy tales on their daddy's lap, they believe. They know that out there somewhere is their knight in shining armor and when the time is right he will ride up, slay the dragon, and defeat the ugly old witch who longs to look just like they do!

Then they grow up, and perhaps their first boyfriend tarnishes the image a little. Things are never quite the same again.

I never wanted to be rescued. At least that's what I told myself. I wanted to be the one doing the rescuing. I know now life had taught me not to look for a rescuer—no one was coming, so I'd better take care of myself.

In a strange reversal of fortunes, however, I am now the one who believes. Yes, at fifty-one, I believe in the most wonderful fairy tale of all—which, as it turns out, is a true story. I believe that I am loved and pursued by the greatest Prince who ever lived. I believe he sees me as I am and loves me completely. I believe now that, as my friend Max Lucado says, I have never lived an unloved moment in my life.

No, this is not some kind of female midlife crisis. I think I have a fairly healthy awareness of what's going on in the world. I don't believe that because I love Jesus I will be spared from pain and sorrow. I don't believe all my prayers will be answered as I would like them to be. I know that I should exercise more, but now at fifty-two I've probably left it too late, and quite honestly I don't have the motivation to get into "the best shape of my life." But who cares! I have a total 100 percent belief that God is in control, and he is watching over me. Do I still have moments of doubt? Sure. But the voice in those moments is far less convincing than it used to be.

Now the question is . . . what about you?

With Christ as my guide, I have been able to face the truth about my past and not just accept it but embrace it. You can do the same. You *deserve* the same. Every painful step on our various journeys has led us to where we are today, and I for one celebrate that.

Now, in case you are tempted to look in the mirror to check

your "princess eligibility" or beauty-queen statistics (in other words, if you're trying to see this from a physical standpoint rather than a spiritual one), I have a caveat to add here. I have a theory about our earthly form. I have absolutely no scripture to back it up, but I'm going to share it anyway and you can do with it what you will! How we view ourselves determines how far we believe we can progress on this spiritual journey. If we see ourselves as "less than" every other woman around, we will hold back and not fully live the life that Christ died to give us. If we understand that on the outside we express in various ways the brokenness of a fallen world but internally we are being redeemed every single day, it could change everything.

I think that each of us is in disguise. No matter what we look like at the moment, God sees that we still look like daughters of Eve. I don't think it matters whether you are a size 2 or a size 2X, whether you are blonde or gray, tall or short. I think our bodies are just an earthly manifestation of the fact that our planet is fallen. I also think they teach us a lot about who we are and what we value.

When you see a woman who is morbidly obese, do you judge her? When you see someone who is so thin her flesh is almost translucent, do you put her in a category of "one of *those* girls"? Do you find yourself looking critically at another's hairstyle or clothing choice or any other physical aspect? Do you do the same with yourself? Perhaps instead—until we all get home and are seen for who we really are—every outward manifestation of what might seem less than perfect can arouse our compassion and care. Our brokenness shows in different ways. Yes, with some of us it shows up in our flesh. But what shows on the outside is of little importance compared to God's quest for our hearts. God doesn't want us to spend our lives looking in the rearview mirror or superglued to what appears to be true now, but rather by faith looking to the view ahead.

I don't know where you are in your spiritual journey. I don't know whether you are at a place in your life where you can honestly say you trust God or if that seems risky to you. Perhaps my portrayal of God's love for you seems too good to be true. If so, I'm here to tell you this is no fairy tale. Just ask Hagar.

the least likely princess

Hagar's story is found in the book of Genesis, chapters 16 though 21. Hagar was a woman with no home of her own and no rights. Even her name meant "fugitive." It is widely accepted that Hagar was a slave Abraham and Sarah picked up during their stay in Egypt. She was there to do as Sarah wished and never question her mistress, no matter how outrageous her demands might be.

You may recall that God promised Abraham in Genesis 12 that he would have descendants as numerous as the dust of the earth. But as time went on and no children were forthcoming, Sarah decided to take things into her own hands. It seemed impossible to her now, in her advanced age, that she would conceive a child; so she told her slave, Hagar, to sleep with her husband.

Reading this from a Western twenty-first-century perspective, this plan seems immoral as well as desperately foolish, but at that time such an undertaking was permissible. In the days and times in which they lived, before God gave Moses the Ten Commandments, the people abided by acceptable laws of the day, one of which was the Code of Hammurabi. In this Babylonian code, one clause stated:

> If a man take a wife and she give this man a maid-servant as wife and she bear him children, and then this maid assume equality with the wife: because she has borne him children her master shall

not sell her for money, but he may keep her as a slave, reckoning her among the maid-servants.

Hagar had no options. She slept with Abraham and became pregnant. Even though this had been Sarah's idea, when Sarah saw this younger woman pregnant by her husband, the sight tormented Sarah. Hagar was not discreet about her joy, either, which only rubbed salt into Sarah's open wounds.

Genesis 16 is a short chapter, but it is very sad. It recounts how Sarah refused to wait for God's perfect plan and so gave birth to the most bitter rivalry in history—the battle between Arab and Jew that still tears at our world today.

Chapter 16 also tells of Hagar's misery as she ran away, pregnant and alone, into the desert. Not much of a fairy tale. But the story doesn't end there. As Hagar struggled alone in the wilderness, an angel of God appeared to her. He told her to go back to Sarah and put up with whatever abuses the now-jealous Sarah inflicted on her. The angel promised Hagar that her son would be the first in a great nation of people. Hagar called God *El Roi*, which means "the God who sees."

If you compare the first fifteen chapters in Genesis with Hagar's story, you'll see how deeply personal the encounter is between Hagar and God's messenger. For Hagar, a slave girl, to be able to call Jehovah God "the One who sees me" is striking. This is the first time in Scripture that God was called by such a personal name.

Hagar went back to the home of Abraham and Sarah and gave birth to Ishmael. Don't you find it interesting that she did as the angel said? I think that when we know God is with us, we can endure most things. It's only when we feel as if we are alone that we lose hope.

Fourteen more years would pass before Sarah became pregnant

and gave birth to Isaac. I can't imagine what the tension must have been like for Hagar and Sarah during those fourteen years, but I know Hagar must have held on to the fact that God cared for her enough to find her broken and alone and give her a path back home to a place where she could have her son.

You know the story doesn't end there. When Abraham turned one hundred years old, Sarah gave birth to Isaac. Now that she was finally a mother, Sarah did not want her slave and "imposter" child under her roof. So Hagar and Ishmael were once more sent out into the desert alone with bread and one skin full of water (Genesis 21). They wandered until they had run out of food and water and were very close to death. Ishmael was so weak Hagar laid him under a bush to die. She walked a short distance from him and sat down and wept what have to be the bitterest tears a mother can shed, thinking about the impending death of her only child.

The Genesis record tells us that God heard the boy cry and sent an angel to Hagar. He told her to take the boy by the hand, for God's promises were not derailed by human circumstances. As she stood, a well appeared. Hagar and Ishmael were able to find fresh water, and they were saved.

I don't know if you are an art lover, but in the Metropolitan Museum of Art in New York there is a beautiful oil painting called *Hagar in the Wilderness*, by French painter Jean-Baptiste-Camille Corot. If you go online and enter the name of the painting into your search engine, you will see this magnificent depiction of God's provision for one mother and her son. In the picture, the boy is lying as if dead at his mother's feet. She has covered her eyes with one hand, and the other is raised in despair. There is such emotion in this beautiful work. As I look at it, I feel her pain and hopelessness. She has nowhere left to go and cannot bear to watch her beloved boy die. What we get to see that Hagar cannot at that moment is that in the upper left-hand corner of the painting, an angel of the Lord is on his way to rescue mother and son.

mercy

One of the things I love most about Hagar's story is the mercy God extended to her. The past was the past, but God gave her a future. To everyone else around her Hagar was a nobody, but not to God.

If you are a woman who feels forgotten, I pray that Hagar's story will help you see God never forgets you. Hagar fled to the desert, in a sense removing herself from the only help or hope that seemed available to a slave girl. Life moved on for Abraham and Sarah. No search party was sent out to find the young woman. She was left by this world to die—but she was not forgotten by heaven. The God who sees never took his eyes off Hagar.

And he never takes his eyes off you.

Scripture is full of stories of women who met God and were never the same again. Whether it was Ruth, who found God out of her desire to honor her mother-in-law, or Rahab, who is described in the Bible as a harlot but recognized the God of Israel as God indeed, God gave them a future. Not only that, but Rahab gave birth to Boaz, who married Ruth. Ruth gave birth to Obed, who was Jesse's father, who in turn was the father of King David. These two women, Rahab and Ruth, are in the lineage of Christ quoted by Matthew in his gospel (1:5). Quite a future!

In his book *Every Woman of the Bible*, Dr. Herbert Lockyer wrote that some theologians have tried to say the Rahab mentioned in the line of Christ cannot have been the one who was a harlot, appalled that such a one would be linked with the Son of God. He said, "Although man's sense of refinement may be shocked, the fact remains that Rahab, Tamar and Bathsheba were sinful women who were purged by God and had their share in the royal line from which Jesus sprang."[1]

In other words, God forgave their pasts and blessed their futures.

How much of your life have you spent looking in the rearview mirror of your story? You may have had an unhappy childhood and have never been able to let go of wishing things had been different. Whether it was an irrational mother or an indifferent father, you still feel the wounds deeply. Are you trapped in the "It *should* have been different" place? If so, I have great empathy for you.

We all long to know we are loved and valued. The fact remains, however, that no one on this planet is completely whole, and therefore no one can live perfectly. But spending too much time looking in the rearview mirror can lead to a wreck.

Perhaps for you today it is time to let go of what you wish was true and accept what is true. No matter how difficult life has been, God in his wisdom placed each one of us in our unique place and time. At times, like Hagar, our circumstances might seem bleak. But I am learning to trust that God knows what he is doing. When the water around me appears to dry up, all I have to do is call on his name, and he will bring refreshment and strength for the next part of the journey.

deliverance discovered

1. What events or disappointments in your past are holding you back?
2. What part of Hagar's story resonated with you? Why?
3. Do you believe God is watching over you at all times? If not, why not?
4. What event or circumstance in your past are you willing to let go of in order to move on?

a prayer of deliverance

Father God,

As I look back at my past, there are many things I don't fully understand. But I thank you that even when I couldn't see your hand you were watching over me. Give me eyes to see you and ears to hear your voice today. Show me what I need to let go of so that I can walk on with you.

In Jesus' name, amen.

FIVE

the trap of unforgiveness

He that demands mercy, and shows none, ruins the bridge over which he himself is to pass.

—Thomas Adams

Life lived without forgiveness becomes a prison.

—William Arthur Ward

Satan's most successful maneuver in churches and Christian organizations is to get people angry at one another; to attack and insult our brothers and sisters, thus splitting the body of Christ.

—Dr. James Dobson

Our Father in heaven,
Hallowed be Your name.
Your kingdom come.
Your will be done on earth as it is in heaven.
Give us this day our daily bread.
And forgive us our debts, as we forgive our debtors.
And do not lead us into temptation, but deliver us from the evil one.

—Matthew 6:9–13

Late in the evening was the only time she would put Mara down. She would place her carefully by the side of her bed where she could still see her. She used to pray before climbing into bed, down on her knees on the floor. But Mara took up too much space and disrupted her thoughts, so she had stopped some time ago. Besides, she had Mara to talk to.

Most nights she slept through until morning, but there were nights when she couldn't rest, and she would pick Mara up again and hold her. Mara liked to hear the same story over and over again. It was "their" story. She used to tell others, but it had become clear after time that people tired of her tale. She and Mara never did.

Someone had even suggested it was time for her to get rid of Mara and move on with her life. She was horrified, for Mara *was* her life. If she got rid of her for good, what would be left?

She found it interesting to see how her life with Mara had changed her reflection in the mirror. It seemed that carrying Mara had caused her shoulders to stoop. As they went over their story time after time, the telling had left marks around her eyes and mouth. It seemed only fitting to her that there would be physical evidence of internal damage. People might not want to hear her story, but they had to see her face.

Just before she turned off her lamp, she looked again at the verse she had inscribed in the front of her Bible.

> She said to them, "Do not call me Naomi; call me Mara, for the Almighty has dealt very bitterly with me." (Ruth 1:20)

a long unforgiveness

I remember my first day of high school with chilling clarity. I woke up that morning excited and a little nervous about going to the "big" school. My brand-new uniform was hanging on the bedroom chair—navy blue blazer, gray skirt, white shirt, and navy-and-gold-striped tie. I put on each item with care and surveyed the new me in the mirror. I liked how I looked.

After a quick breakfast, I headed to the bus stop. My elementary school had been within walking distance, but the high school was a few miles away, so this was my first ride on the school bus. As I sat on one of the wide seats listening to the chatter of other students, I looked at everything in my satchel for the fiftieth time. My pencil case was full of freshly sharpened pencils and a new eraser, and my notebooks all had my name carefully inscribed. I had a snack in case I got hungry, and I had saved a little of my allowance for the school's concession store (in case the snack was not enough!). I was all set to go.

But before the bus could reach the school, rain began to pelt against the windows. I was disappointed—I didn't want my new blazer to get wet. (When it rains in Scotland, it is never a faint thing; it is a full-on attack.) I'd have to make a run for it when the bus arrived.

Finally the bus pulled in, and we students tumbled out into the rain with satchels over our heads. I ran as quickly as I could with my head down, trying not to get mud on my "sensible" black lace-up shoes and my new white socks. I fell in behind the group and began to follow the legs in front of me. We reached the door and ran inside.

But when I lowered the satchel from over my head and looked around, I froze on the spot. *Green* blazers surrounded me—not a navy one in sight. Our school stood side by side with the Catholic school, and I had obviously followed the wrong legs!

Now, if you were born and raised in America, it might be hard to understand why this incident was so shocking. But in Scotland and Ireland—particularly at that time—there existed a violent hatred between Protestants and Catholics. We were kept strictly apart in schools and in the sections of town where we lived.

The bloody hostility that erupted in Northern Ireland in the mid-1960s was in essence a resurgence of the hatred that had existed for several hundred years between Protestants and Catholics, going all the way back to the seventeenth century. At the beginning of the 1970s, British armed forces moved in, essentially as a peace-keeping force, but the violence only escalated. One of my most poignant memories of that time is of watching the news one night while young children threw rocks at soldiers. The children couldn't have been older than five or six, but the expressions on their faces were chilling. A reporter thrust a microphone in front of one of the children and asked her why she was throwing rocks at the soldiers.

"Because I hate them," she said.

The reporter asked why.

"Because my mammy told me I do."

Hate and bitterness are contagious. Think of the countless countries that still deal with civil unrest, whether for religious or other reasons. Look at the racial tension and hatred that are still alive here in America. The trouble with that kind of deep-seated bitterness is that no amount of revenge is ever enough. For every blow struck by one side, the other retaliates with a fresh one, and the cycle continues. There is never enough blood spilled to wash away the bitterness.

But as devastating as unforgiveness is on a national or tribal level, it is lethal to the individual.

the path to pain

From Genesis to Revelation, the golden thread of forgiveness is woven through the Word of God as the key to deliverance. When we are unable to forgive or refuse to forgive, we become hostages to the pain of the past. Just like the woman in the parable, bitterness can ruin our lives, poisoning the soul. We can hold on to it until it's hard for us to know where we end and where the bitter unforgiveness begins. We become one as the negativity warps our sense of self.

Alongside our emotional and spiritual well-being, bitterness has a direct impact on our physical health. Sometimes it feels as though the anger and unforgiveness we carry inside twist our bodies, affecting our lives in a multitude of ways—including illness. Doctors know this. In the October 27, 1997, issue of *Archives of Internal Medicine*, the editors asked physicians, "What specific personality characteristic causes physical illness?" Their answer: anger.[1]

This is not a new belief. According to the Torah and other Jewish literature, the gallbladder is thought to be the seat of all diseases. In Hebrew, the word for gallbladder is *marah*, meaning "bitter." The word *marah* is also given a numerical value—*machalah*, meaning "eighty-three." Jewish culture believes the root of the eighty-three illnesses that afflict mankind come from the gallbladder, which, when stressed by unresolved anger and bitterness, produces too much bile. Think about the last time you were angry, your stomach tightening and roiling in physical reaction, and you get the idea.

Scripture is full of stories of those whose lives were ruined by anger and bitterness, both emotionally and physically. For instance, if we look at the very first family, we see the devastation that deep-seated resentment can cause. It took the life of one man and splintered a whole family.

Eve gave birth to two boys, Cain and Abel. And as in most families, the children's gifts and personalities were very different.

> Now Abel was a keeper of sheep, but Cain was a tiller of the ground. And in the process of time it came to pass that Cain brought an offering of the fruit of the ground to the Lord. Abel also brought of the firstborn of his flock and of their fat. And the Lord respected Abel and his offering, but He did not respect Cain and his offering. And Cain was very angry, and his countenance fell. So the Lord said to Cain, "Why are you angry? And why has your countenance fallen? If you do well, will you not be accepted? And if you do not do well, sin lies at the door. And its desire *is* for you, but you should rule over it." (Genesis 4:2–7)

God warned Cain what unresolved anger can do, but Cain ignored the warning: "Cain rose up against Abel his brother and killed him" (v. 8).

That kind of anger doesn't come in a moment. It begins in little ways that are left unchecked. I wonder how many of those moments existed for Cain as a child. Perhaps he felt Eve favored his brother or that Adam gave a better gift to Abel than to him one day. Like an overpacked suitcase, Cain's anger grew until he could no longer contain it; and in a moment, he changed the lives of four people.

When that much venom exists, it has to go somewhere. Before Christ's sacrifice on Calvary, someone had to pay the price. In this case, it was Abel. And Cain as well. If Cain had simply been able to let go of his angry feelings, rather than allowing them to fester for who knows how long, his brother would have lived and Cain himself might have had a prosperous and fulfilling life. Instead, he was banished (Genesis 4:11–16). I wonder if he felt his unforgiveness was worth that price.

why is it so hard to forgive?

"But Sheila," you ask, "if forgiveness is so important to the life of a believer, then why is it so hard?" You're not alone. I can think of many similar comments I have heard from others. A few of the usual ones include:

- Fear: "What if I forgive and they do it again?"
- Mistrust: "I've heard it all before, and I don't believe they're really sorry."
- Pain: "How can saying 'I forgive you' take away the deep wound inside?"
- Bitterness: "Nothing can change what happened to me."

Let's take a look at each of these feelings and how they affect us.

"what if i forgive and they do it again?"

Forgiveness means we surrender our right to know the outcome. That is hard. We want to know that if we forgive, then the person will be sorry and never hurt us again. When we forgive someone and he turns right round and does the same thing again, not only are we wounded afresh, but we feel so foolish. That never sits well with us.

I was at my bank a few days ago, waiting in line to deposit a check, when I became aware of negotiations taking place between two brothers just ahead of me. One must have been about six and the other, four. It went a little like this:

"Come on, Sam, let me hold your sucker. I promise I won't eat it."

"But you said that last time."

"I know, but I mean it this time."

"All right."

And then soon after:

"Mom! He ate my sucker!"

"Well, why did you give it to him?"

I felt so sorry for this poor kid. Not only had he trusted his brother a second time, but he had been made to feel that it was his fault for believing the best.

Life is hard! And uncertain. But we have access to a Father who can comfort us when the bullies and deceivers come, and when we feel like dunces for the mistakes we make. It may take time for trust and healing to begin . . . or finish. But God is patient. He never said life would be easy; he said he would be there for us—in the good decisions and the bad.

"i've heard it all before, and i don't believe they're really sorry"

Another reason we struggle with forgiveness is because we have cheapened what forgiveness really is. There is an element of sentimentality among many in the evangelical church who would suggest forgiveness is easy and quick. People apply forgiveness like a Band-Aid over a wound, without recognizing the wound has to be addressed, acknowledged, grieved over, and owned before forgiveness can ever be real and lasting. To minimize someone's pain with a "Hey, I'm sorry, friend" and even a quick prayer—without truly acknowledging any wrongdoing and its heartfelt consequences—is an offense in itself. It can tarnish our faith in someone and make us slow to accept forgiveness.

In reality, we may never receive a true apology from our offender. Honestly, though, what good is gained in allowing our wound to fester? Do we feel better for having wrapped ourselves up in our anger? More important, does it enhance our relationships with others and with God?

Jesus said, "In prayer there is a connection between what God does and what you do. You can't get forgiveness from God, for instance, without also forgiving others. If you refuse to do your part, you cut yourself off from God's part" (Matthew 6:14–15 MSG).

The message is very clear: if we want to live free in Christ's love, we must forgive. I believe that getting to that place makes a huge difference in the integrity of our souls and the depth of forgiveness and healing we experience. And I think we need to honestly examine our response in light of any offense against us.

"how can saying 'i forgive you' take away the deep wound inside?

I decided one day to go through my closet and "seasonalize" it. Although it was only May, the weather in Dallas was already in the nineties, so it was time to put away winter coats and sweaters. They had served their purpose for the twelve days a year when the temperature gets below seventy here.

As I worked, it became clear to me that I needed some new lightweight clothes. So when I finished, I hopped in my car and headed for the mall. I came home with four T-shirts and two summer sweaters, which I then tried on and asked Barry what he thought.

He looked at me and paused.

I turned around so that he could get a better look.

He smiled and said, "That's a nice color."

His hesitation was palpable. Then he asked, "Did they have a bigger size?"

I told him that these fit perfectly and he had no idea what he was talking about.

He said he was sorry and they looked fine.

All that day I walked around with a little growling dog inside me. Several times I snapped at Barry's heels until I finally had to own what was true: he had really hurt my feelings and fed into some old wounds.

Now on the surface, this might seem like a little thing. Goodness knows many women have dealt with husbands who can't seem to "get" the Rule of Opinion: if your wife asks how she looks, for goodness' sake tell her she looks fabulous! But as I've written elsewhere in this book (and others), I struggled greatly in the past with overeating as compensation for some very deep hurts in my life. For Barry to suggest my clothes were too tight connected with my past struggle with my weight. I was losing not just the battle with my figure but an emotional battle too.

It took my admitting my fears and Barry's sincere apology to begin to heal that pain. He looked me in the eyes and told me he was really sorry and asked me to forgive him. And prayerfully asking God for strength, I was able to let it go.

I know that is a small example; I know many of you struggle with daily hurts far beyond a husband's thoughtless comment. But the principle holds good through the gamut of human emotions. I believe we can only really forgive when we acknowledge the depth to which we have been wounded and allow ourselves to "own" the pain. By "own" the pain, I mean face the truth that we are wounded. It is tempting to slough pain away, denying we are hurt. It can be embarrassing to be wounded. We feel weak or out of control. So we ignore it.

We need to accept that we live in a world where at times pain is just part of the package. When we humbly admit that we are wounded and allow ourselves to feel that pain, only then can we bring it to Christ for healing and begin the process of forgiveness.

"nothing can change what happened to me"

The other day I was at the supermarket, standing in the "ten items or less" line—which, as we all know, is trouble waiting to happen. The man at the front of the line had eleven items in his cart. I only know that because the woman standing immediately behind him counted them out loud for all to hear. The man seemed genuinely embarrassed and offered to put something back, but the checkout girl had the common decency to tell him that wasn't necessary.

This only further ignited the fury of the Offended One. She used a bucket of verbal water to put out a solitary match. I imagine she went home and bickered about the incident all evening, slipping into bed that night with thoughts of revenge on the hapless fellow who dared disobey.

But let's pull back the drapes a little and see what might have been taking place inside this woman that led her to unload on this unsuspecting shopper. What if this woman has been piling up grievances over the days, weeks, and years? What if not all of them are small? Perhaps at some point in her life, this woman was seriously wronged by someone, yet she never received the healing of forgiveness—was never able to let her pain go for fear it would diminish the wrongs against her. In such a situation, where negativity begins to take over, transgressions big and small can begin to pile up until something as small as eleven items in a ten-and-under grocery line is enough to put you over the edge. If she has been stepped on time after time, the message that plays in her head is, *Nothing will ever change—once a victim always a victim.*

How many times, dear reader, have you found yourself grousing at someone, knowing full well the real reason for your discontent is another matter entirely? Have you ever truly examined your heart for hurts you tend to shove under the carpet rather than let go of? I know I have. Sometimes I find myself firing off at little things because there is something far deeper I have not dealt with. All it does in the end is add to the pile.

Do we want to be like Cain, who allowed his anger to destroy not only his own life but his brother's? Do we want to be like the grocery store woman, who allowed something as small as an extra box of cereal to ruin her day? Or do we want to let go of our frustration, trusting that the God who sees all will take care of things in his own time?

If we are going to forgive—if we're going to bring our pain to Christ—we have to relinquish the right to "get even."

the many colors of forgiveness

Depending on how personal our wounds are, letting go can be very hard. Let's be honest: it's human nature to want to hurt the one who hurts. So often we hold on to our unforgiveness because we just can't relinquish the idea of retribution—whether honestly deserved or not. But, as we know, God claims vengeance for himself (Deuteronomy 32:35). As hard as it is to admit, it's not really up to us to expect a feel-good ending for all our woes. We simply have to trust that justice will take its God-ordained course.

That doesn't mean Christians should be wishy-washy when it comes to what is right and what is wrong. We are called to stand up for righteousness. We don't excuse the behavior of the offender, nor do we expect that forgiveness removes the consequences of a person's actions. A friend unjustly maligned can choose to let bygones be bygones, but that doesn't mean the transgressor should be allowed to continue with a hurtful attitude. A battered wife who reports her husband's abuse can choose for the sake of her soul to forgive him, but that does not mean he should go unpunished for his crime under the laws of our country.

I once spoke with a woman who was deeply disturbed after being told by members of her church that if she forgave her abusive husband, she should return to him. This—what I believe to be faulty theology—put her in an internal prison. She wanted to be able to forgive him, but she was afraid to because then she would have to go back and potentially face more abuse. He was not in any kind of counseling or accountability group, so there was no reason for her to believe that he had changed. I believe that in situations like this, forgiveness is offered to set us free, not to put a Band-Aid over the gross sin of another.

When I was the cohost of *The 700 Club* with Dr. Pat Robertson, one of the stories we covered revealed the lives of some of the men and women in the infamous Charles Manson "family." You may remember that on August 9, 1969, several members of the Manson "family" murdered five people in Los Angeles. One was actress Sharon Tate, who was eight and a half months pregnant. She begged for the life of her unborn son, but the murderers showed no mercy.

The following evening, the same killers broke into the home of Rosemary and Leno LaBianca and murdered both of them. Their daughter, Susan, was the one who discovered their bodies. The horror of what she saw caused her to have a complete breakdown.

Charles "Tex" Watson, reputedly one of the most brutal of the killers, received the death penalty, but in 1972 that was overturned and he was sentenced to life imprisonment. Three years later, he prayed with the prison chaplain and gave his life to Christ. Today he is serving out his sentence in Mule Creek state prison. He is married with four children and is an ordained minister. He has applied for parole thirteen times, and each time it has been denied.

What is pertinent to us here is the presence of two women at the parole hearings. One is the LaBiancas' daughter, Susan. The other is Patti Tate, Sharon Tate's younger sister. Susan is a believer and has visited Tex Watson in prison. In her heart, she believes he has genuinely repented and she has forgiven him. When she appeared at the parole hearing in 1990, it was to make a plea for Watson to be released.

Patti Tate, on the other hand, was present at the hearing to demand that he be kept in prison. Her mother, who has since passed, spent the rest of her life making sure the Manson murderers were never let out. She went on record saying, "There is no connection between faith and release."

In many ways, both women are still chained to the event that changed their lives forever. Having never lived through the horror of such events, it is hard to imagine how one would cope and even begin to move on with life; but here is what I believe about the gift of forgiveness. Forgiveness unclenches our fists and allows us to let go. It says to God, "I cannot change what happened, although everything inside me cries out for justice. I don't believe that true justice exists anymore on this earth, so I am placing this unspeakable situation into your hands. I don't have to make offenders suffer, and I don't have to make them feel better about themselves. I relinquish them to you, and today, right now in Jesus' name, I choose life."

The cost of unforgiveness can rob a human heart of all joy and hope. It can trap someone in circumstances that took place years before as if caught in a time warp. But until the day we stand before the throne and see the Lamb of God face-to-face, forgiveness is God's gift to us to heal our hearts and set us free. Dear reader, you *can* be delivered of bitterness and unforgiveness. It doesn't matter how long you have held on to it or how it has shaped your life up until this point. I believe with all my heart that in Jesus' name you can be free.

deliverance discovered

1. Who has wounded your heart?
2. When you think of that person or situation, how does it make you feel?
3. Do you want to be healed from this pain?
4. Write a short prayer, asking God to help you relinquish the right to get even.

a prayer of deliverance

Father God,

I come to you in the powerful name of Jesus. You alone know the bitterness and unforgiveness I have held on to for so long. Father, I want to be free. I want to be healed so that I can love you with my whole heart.

I renounce my right to get even. I surrender my heart and my will to you. I choose to forgive, no matter how I feel. Thank you for the gift of your Holy Spirit to lead me into all truth.

In Jesus' name, amen.

SIX

don't play fair—it will set you free

As we practice the work of forgiveness we discover more and more that forgiveness and healing are one.

—Agnes Sanford

Life lived without forgiveness becomes a prison.

—William Arthur Ward

He has not dealt with us according to our sins,
Nor punished us according to our iniquities.
For as the heavens are high above the earth,
So great is His mercy toward those who fear Him.
As far as the east is from the west,
So far has He removed our transgressions from us.

—Psalm 103:10–12

I, even I, am He who blots out your transgressions for My own sake;
And I will not remember your sins.

—Isaiah 43:25

let go

If we say that we have no sin, we deceive ourselves, and the truth is not in us. If we confess our sins, He is faithful and just to forgive us our sins and to cleanse us from all unrighteousness.

—1 John 1:8–9

Forgiving, when you come down to it, is an art, a practical art, maybe the most neglected of all the healing arts. It is the art of healing inner wounds inflicted by other people's wrongs.

—Lewis Smedes

The cage sat in a pretty part of the house. It was by a window where the bird could see blue sky and puffy white clouds racing across the sky on a windy day. Some mornings, other birds would sit on the window ledge and talk to her.

"Good morning!" they said one afternoon. "How are you this fine day?"

"I am very well," she replied. "How is life in the open sky?"

"Yesterday was windy, which was very fun," one bird said. "When the wind blows just right, it's as if you only have to think of flying and you can soar and spin and dive toward the sea."

"I cannot remember what that feels like anymore," the bird said. "It has been so long since I've felt the wind under my wings."

"May I ask her, Mama?" a young bird whispered.

"You may," her mother replied.

"Ma'am," the bird began, "why do you live in this cage? The cage door is open and yet I have never seen you step outside."

"It is because of my broken wing," the bird replied. "Some time ago, one of the dark ones attacked me in the air, and I have not been able to fly since."

"Are you afraid that if you go outside you might see him again?" the bird asked.

"No, little one," she replied. "I am not afraid anymore. I have forgiven him. I am just broken."

"May I tell her, Mama?" the young one asked.

"You may."

"Ma'am, I think if you tried it, you would see your wing has been whole for quite some time now," the little bird said.

"Do you believe so?" she replied. "I wonder . . ."

"I *do* believe so, ma'am," the little one said emphatically.

So the bird stepped from her cage, stretched her wings, and took to the air.

"Look at her fly, Mama! Look at her fly!"

taken to a prison to be set free

In the fall of 2007, I received an e-mail from a woman who had attended a Women of Faith conference in Little Rock, Arkansas, where I had spoken. She told me there was a women's prison just a few miles from Little Rock and wondered if the next time I visited the city I could include an evening at the prison. I was glad to say yes. I knew I would be back in April, so I wrote it in my calendar.

When the day came, she picked me up at my hotel and we drove the few miles to the facility. As we approached the ominous barbed-wire fence, I asked her to fill me in on what she knew about the inmates. She told me she volunteered in a unit in the prison where fifty women were part of program called the Inner Change Freedom Initiative. This program was established by Prison Fellowship as an intense, values-based program taught from a biblical perspective.

Inmates sign up for eighteen months, and after their release they are given help to reintegrate into society.

I met some of the prison staff and was escorted to the large hall where I would speak. Two of the inmates were assigned to help run my CD track so I could sing a couple of songs as well. They were sweet, kind women with quite a sense of humor. When I saw there were candles sitting on the podium, I asked one of the inmates if I should light them.

She replied, "Don't ask me. I'm in here for arson!"

As the other inmates began to pour in, I watched their faces. They looked like they could have been my sisters or friends. I knew that some were in for first- or second-degree murder, and many for drug-related offenses or theft. Yet without fear, I made my way down the rows of women, shaking hands or sharing a hug.

I will never forget that night. I spoke on freedom and forgiveness—that true freedom is not the absence of bars but the very real presence of Christ. As the theme verse for the Freedom Initiative's ministry states, "Therefore, if anyone is in Christ, he is a new creation; old things have passed away; behold, all things have become new" (2 Corinthians 5:17). These women were living examples. As I sang at the end of my message, women stood with their arms stretched out to God in worship, tears pouring down their faces. The presence of Christ was so apparent with these broken women, I couldn't help but think of the psalmist's words: "The sacrifice you want is a broken spirit. A broken and repentant heart, O God, you will not despise" (Psalm 51:17 NLT).

Afterward, the assistant warden was kind enough to let me spend some one-on-one time with some of the inmates. As I listened to their stories, two things became very clear: (1) forgiveness has the power to heal the most brutal of wounds, and (2) the most difficult person to forgive can be the one we see in the mirror every morning.

the most brutal of wounds

One of the greatest saints of Christian history began as one of its greatest persecutors—Saul of Tarsus, who became Paul the apostle. We read in Acts 8:3, "As for Saul, he made havoc of the church, entering every house, and dragging off men and women, committing them to prison." It was Saul's committed intent to destroy the church.

We read on in chapter 9: "Then Saul, still breathing threats and murder against the disciples of the Lord, went to the high priest and asked letters from him to the synagogues of Damascus, so that if he found any who were of the Way, whether men or women, he might bring them bound to Jerusalem" (vv. 1–2).

Saul had no idea he was about to be knocked from his horse by the blinding light of the living Christ. But that's what happened one day on the way to Damascus. He heard a voice saying, "Saul, Saul, why are you persecuting Me?" (v. 4). Saul was greatly confounded. He asked, "Who are You, Lord?"

Saul knew this had to be a message from God (in Acts 26:13, he wrote that the light of Christ was brighter than the light of the sun), but God's question made no sense to him. As far as Saul was concerned, he wasn't persecuting God but rather was defending true Judaism.

Then Jesus spoke: "I am Jesus, whom you are persecuting" (Acts 9:5).

Can you even begin to imagine the shock? Saul had just been told Jesus Christ really was the Messiah and he, Saul, was destroying Jesus' people.

After his conversion, Saul had to be introduced to the disciples and other believers. He had to come face-to-face with those whose families he had devastated through his actions. How could they forgive such a grievous wound?

We read in Acts 9:26, "When Saul had come to Jerusalem, he tried to join the disciples; but they were all afraid of him, and did not believe that he was a disciple." It had to be a huge hurdle to embrace the fact that this man, who was known for his hatred and cruelty against Christians, was now a brother. I wonder how many struggled with his conversion, perhaps not doubting its validity but questioning the justice of such a gift.

But a brother in Christ he was. And Saul—now named Paul—went on to become a great leader and hero of the early church. The passion that had once led him to persecute now led him to love. His remorse was as clear as day. And his brothers' forgiveness of him was justified and rewarded a thousand times over.

I believe when we have been deeply wounded by someone—including someone who is not remotely remorseful—forgiveness is the salve that heals us. We don't even need to voice it to the person. It can be a transaction between God and us.

One of the ladies at the prison gave me a letter. In it, she told me her story. It was a heartbreaking tale of sexual and physical abuse much worse than anything I had ever heard described before. What impacted me was what she shared as she concluded her story. She said that "God took me to a prison to set me free."

In past books, I've shared about my voluntary admittance to a psychiatric hospital. So many times I have used that same phrase—God took me to a prison to set me free—when trying to explain what a gift that one-month stay was for me. In a place of confinement I had to stop running long enough to come face-to-face with my depression and throw myself into the arms of God's love. To hear a dear sister who carried on her body and in her soul bruises and scars etched on her by the cruelty of others describe her journey in the same ten words was beyond humbling. I cannot begin to imagine her pain.

And yet just as I met the risen Christ in the midst of my darkest night, so did she.

Some of the people who wounded her are gone from this earth. Some refuse to acknowledge their guilt. But she is no longer a slave to any of them. She took her wounds to Calvary, and even as Christ forgave her for her sins, she forgave those who had sinned against her. And because of that she has been set free—healed from the most brutal of wounds.

I will always remember her face. Although it was lined around the eyes, there was a quiet beauty and calm there. It was the lightness of one whose wings were broken but who now soars again.

the hardest battle of all

Most of us find it hard to forgive ourselves for some of the things we do. Regret is a brutal taskmaster. We lie in bed at night, beating ourselves up with what-ifs and if-onlys and despising our weak natures. While I don't think we need to needlessly castigate ourselves with unnecessary guilt, I don't think it's necessarily a bad thing when we find it hard to forgive ourselves. I don't think it should be easy.

Before you start writing me letters asking why I can't simply accept God's forgiveness, let me explain myself! When I have done something to wound another or to offend God, I think it is only appropriate that I should wrestle with that. Grace is free, but it is not cheap. It cost Christ everything to open the very throne room of heaven to us, so when I am in need of forgiveness, I should not come skipping in like it's no skin off my back.

We live in a world of quick fixes and instant gratification where we have an immediate answer to a felt need. But what works well for drive-through restaurants does not serve our spirits well. Jesus told his followers they would know the truth, and the truth would set them free (John 8:32). It is tempting to rush straight to the freedom part and miss out knowing the truth. But if I want to experience true freedom from whatever wrongs I have committed, I need to face what I did and then separate it from who I am.

The only door to true freedom and forgiveness is to face what we did square in the eye and own it to its full extent. Saul was given three days to sit with his sin before his sight was restored (Acts 9:9). My friend in prison found freedom as she faced the fact that her criminal response to what had been done to her was not the answer. When we are able by God's grace to face the worst that is true about us, we no longer have to fear what might be exposed at any minute.

It's vital, though, that we separate what we did from who we are.

If you are the kind of person, like me, who has ever dealt with shame at a core level, this is for you! How many times have you said to yourself any of the following:

- "I am a bad person."
- "How could I have been so stupid?"
- "I'll never change!"
- "I deserve the bad things that happen to me."
- "If people knew the real me, they would see that I'm a fraud."

That is not appropriate guilt. That is shame, and it does not belong to you as a daughter of the King. I am learning that if I do or say something that is hurtful or unkind, then I did a bad *thing*. I am not a bad *person*.

In *The Art of Forgiving*, Lewis Smedes wrote:

> We forgive ourselves for what we do;
> We accept ourselves as we are,

Sometimes in spite of who we are,
But always *as* we are.[1]

In other words, forgiveness means being comfortable with ourselves, the good and the bad. We don't have to be perfect. What empowering words!

Smedes suggested an exercise that might feel a little funny at first but that has power and a point. He said we should look long and hard at ourselves in the mirror and say, "God forgives you, and so do I." I challenge you to do this. Only when you are truly able to forgive yourself will you be able to live with yourself.

fly away!

I am convinced that forgiveness is the triumph of the believer over the reality that we live on a fallen planet. It is a powerful weapon that overcomes the evil in this world and brings healing to our wounded souls—but we must reach out and accept it. To say that we don't deserve to be forgiven is to make our sin more powerful than the blood of Christ. If God forgives us, then we must forgive ourselves. When we refuse, we have made the court of our opinion or the opinion of others more powerful than the court of an all-knowing and all-powerful God. It must be a serious wound to the heart of our Father when we will not accept the gift he has given us because it cost him so dearly. You were bought with a price, dear sister. Every sin was covered by the lifeblood of the Lamb. To refuse such an offering is a pride that must be laid at the foot of the cross.

Accepting forgiveness with a humble heart does not mean that the marks will disappear. The marks will still be there, but I think they can be seen as gifts when we view them as reminders of the grace and mercy of God to us. Our wings may bear a few scars or broken feathers, but by God's grace and freedom, we will fly.

deliverance discovered

1. How does the story of Paul's conversion impact your understanding of forgiveness?
2. Do you find it harder to forgive others or to forgive yourself? Why?
3. In what ways do you separate guilt and shame in your own life?
4. How can you see your wounds now as marks of the grace of God?

a prayer of deliverance

Father God,

I cannot even begin to understand the depth of everything you have forgiven me of. I thank you and praise you that you have given me a new start and a new heart. I pray that by your grace and through the power of the Holy Spirit, you will give me a fresh understanding of the debt you have paid for me.

I thank you also for the grace to forgive others and for the peace of forgiving myself, so that I might be healed.

In Jesus' name, amen.

SEVEN

the trouble with temptation is that it's just so tempting

'Tis one thing to be tempted, another thing to fall.

—William Shakespeare

Eve, with all the fruits of Eden blest, save only one, rather than leave that one unknown, lost all the rest.

—Thomas Moore

God delights in our temptations and yet hates them. He delights in them when they drive us to prayer; he hates them when they drive us to despair.

—Martin Luther

Now Jesus, full of the Holy Spirit, left the Jordan and was led by the Spirit into the wild. For forty wilderness days and nights he was tested by the Devil.

—Luke 4:1–2 msg

No test or temptation that comes your way is beyond the course of what others have had to face. All you need to remember is that God will never let you down; he'll never let you be pushed past your limit; he'll always be there to help you come through it.

—1 CORINTHIANS 10:13 MSG

The party was going very well. Samantha had questioned herself over and over about the wisdom of having twenty-two six-year-old girls in the house, but so far, so good. She was impressed with the clown she had booked to entertain. If the volume of laughter coming from the den was any indication of success, then Miss Rosebud was a hit!

"Look, Mommy," her daughter cried, bursting into the kitchen. "Miss Rosebud made me a crown out of pink balloons!"

"That's wonderful," Samantha said. "You look like a perfect little princess."

It was time for the cake. She carefully lit the six candles, and on her cue her husband dimmed the lights in the den.

Happy birthday to you.
Happy birthday to you.
Happy birthday, dear Abby.
Happy birthday to you.

Abby closed her eyes, made a wish, and blew out all six candles.

Samantha took the cake back into the kitchen to cut it into six-year-old-girl-sized pieces. Emma, one of Abby's friends, followed her in, saying that she would help. Very carefully Emma delivered a piece of pink princess cake to each girl. But on her last piece, her foot caught in the tulle fabric of her princess party costume, and she fell, dropping the last piece of cake she was to deliver.

"Don't worry, Emma," Samantha said. "As long as you're all right, there's plenty more cake."

Sarah scraped the cake off the kitchen floor onto the paper plate and set it on the edge of the counter.

"I'll take that piece, Mrs. Conner," Emma said.

"Don't be silly, Emma," Samantha said. "No one is going to eat that piece. I think you should get an extra-special big piece for being such a good helper."

While Emma straightened herself up, Samantha cut a big corner piece and then went through to the den to pick up any plates and pieces of cake before the dog helped himself to them. When she came back to the kitchen, Emma was eating the piece of cake that had been scraped up from the floor.

"Emma, why are you eating that piece?" she asked.

"Because you said I couldn't have it," Emma replied.

a tempting offer

The desert can be a cruel place. Barren and hot during the day, bitterly cold at night, empty of sustenance. It's not a place you or I would choose to spend much time—at least not without basic creature comforts. Yet we find more than once that God used the desert for his purposes.

Take the children of Israel. As told in Exodus, following some devastating choices, they ended up wandering around the desert for forty years. They'd just been released from bondage in Egypt and given the promise of a new life. Their story reads like a Shakespearian tragedy. I find myself holding my breath at each turn of the page.

- *Will they get it right this time?*
- *Will they finally choose the right path, or will they take another wrong turn that will lead them deeper and deeper into despair?*
- *Can't they see what they are doing? Will they never learn?*

In their desire for immediate gratification, the Israelites repeatedly turned from God. Time after time they gave in to temptation and suffered the consequences—for forty years!

Jesus, too, had choices to make in the desert. He was led by the Spirit into the wilderness for the specific assignment of being tested by the vicious enemy of his soul. For forty years the Israelites disappointed God, yet after forty days of physical denial Jesus faced the enemy and showed us a new way to live.

Jesus was tested, and he overcame temptation. Every day we struggle to say no to things that trip us up or yes to things we know are right. Why is that? Because like the Israelites, we're selfish. Simply put, we want what we want, and we'd really like it now. It's human nature, and it harkens back to that tasty morsel of fruit in the garden of Eden. Over time and by God's grace we learn to temper our selfish nature, but some vestige of it still lurks under the surface.

Of course, different things tempt each of us. For some of us (okay, a lot of us) it's food. We crave food when we are happy, when we are sad, and when we can't quite make up our minds what we are. We gorge ourselves again and again until we can't move.

For others, it is relationships. We search for the perfect man who will fill the empty space inside us. We demand a certain ideal and won't settle for anything less, even if it means we might spend a lot of time alone.

For some, it is the temptation to dwell on the past and not move on to all that God has for us. Perhaps we feel if we move on we'll be letting go of something that is part of who we are. For many of us, the past is a golden age we grasp for, forgetting all the future might hold for us.

Whatever the temptation, the common thread will be the amount of time and energy involved in dealing with it—which is what Satan wants. A person preoccupied with herself is a person not preoccupied with God.

Satan tempted Jesus in three areas of life we all face on this earth: satisfying immediate felt needs, finding an easy way out of suffering, and giving in to charisma over character. Let's take a closer look at these three temptations.

satisfying immediate felt needs

"I Want It and I Want It Now!"

> "If You are the Son of God, command that these stones become bread." (Matthew 4:3)

Not long ago, I was in the mall quite late picking up a few things before I traveled that weekend. As I stood in line to pay for some hose, I became aware of a "disturbance" at a cash register over in the children's department. A frazzled mom was attempting to pay for her little girl's pink Crocs, but she was obviously taking way too long. The child was pulling at the edge of her mother's sweater and yelling at a volume that could have been heard three counties away, "I want them, and I want them now!"

Bless her sinful little heart.

Her mom finally said to her, "Molly, will you please stop pulling on me and wait for thirty seconds!"

"But I don't want to wait!" was Molly's wail.

I saw myself in this impatient little soul. So many times my prayers must sound just like her demand for instant gratification.

What immediate need did Satan tempt Jesus with? Food.

It was clear Satan had been stalking Christ from the beginning. When Jesus came up from the Jordan River, God had announced, "This is my Son" (Matthew 3:17 MSG). As Satan approached Jesus, now he echoed what he'd heard at the baptism: "If You are the Son . . ." (4:3).

It was a calculated approach. The temptation was real and understandable. Jesus would have been very hungry at the end of forty days without food. (Most reputable books on fasting say forty days is the length of time a man can fast before his body begins to consume healthy muscle and tissue.) If you have ever allowed yourself to become really hungry, you will notice that it is much easier to be irritable and not so clearheaded. An Arabian philosopher gave this piece of advice to his son: "My son, never go out of the house in the morning, till thou hast eaten something: by so doing, thy mind will be more firm; and, shouldest thou be insulted by any person, thou wilt find thyself more disposed to suffer patiently: for hunger dries up and disorders the brain."[1]

Jesus was being tempted with something very basic—something we can all understand and appreciate at gut level. I think that's significant, if for nothing else than it shows us how sneaky Satan is. Rather than tempt Jesus with something overtly evil like lust or murder, Satan appealed to what would seem innocent, innocuous. We all need food to live, and Satan was just offering a little something to tide Jesus over until he could get back to his friends and family and find the nourishment his body needed.

Jesus replied: "It is written: 'Man does not live on bread alone, but on every word that comes from the mouth of God'" (Matthew 4:4 NIV). His response showed an undivided heart. Jesus was in essence redeeming the Law given through Moses to the children of Israel. All the Israelites cared about was what they needed or thought they couldn't have, but Jesus said there are things that matter more. Physical hunger and release are only temporary, but God's plan is eternal.

My family was eating in a restaurant recently, and Barry asked Christian to give thanks for our food. When our waitress came over to fill our water glasses, she said, "It's a long time since I've seen anyone do that in here." What an interesting comment. It's as if we have separated the physical and the spiritual rather than seeing all of life as a gift from God.

Cravings reveal to us what is true and what is false. How many times have you found yourself thinking, *This is what I really need to feel better about myself.* Whether the "this" is food or a new dress or a new relationship, the gratification of the craving reveals that we were longing for something more, something deeper because the satisfaction is so short-lived. Jesus told Satan that bread might satisfy for a moment but to really live, we need the Word of God.

Seeing that Christ refused the opportunity to gratify his immediate needs, Satan moved on to a much more tempting prize. The second temptation, if Christ had succumbed, would have been the end of us all.

finding an easy way out of suffering

The Crown Without the Cross

> All this authority I will give You, and their glory; for this has been delivered to me, and I give it to whomever I wish. Therefore, if You will worship before me, all will be Yours. (Luke 4:6–7)

Satan took Jesus to a high place (Matthew's gospel records it as a mountain). There, in an instant, he showed Jesus all the kingdoms of the world. What he offered was everything that would be Christ's—on one condition. No Calvary. No agony and suffering. There is some debate in theological circles as to whether Satan showed Christ a vision of the entire earth or took him to a mountain where he would be able to cast his eyes over the splendor of all of Judea and some of the surrounding nations. Either way, the sight would be spectacular. Would the sun be rising over the mountains of Arabia or rain gently falling on the plains of Moab? Would the Jordan River be in full spate and the Dead Sea spread before him like a sheet of glass? Remember that Jesus, the Word, spoke this beauty into being; our earth and those of us who walk on it are Christ's passion. Satan was offering the beauty of it all without the barbaric death that lay just three short years ahead.

Now on a simple surface read, Satan's offer might seem like a perfect idea: absolute authority rather than death. Yet Satan and Jesus both knew there was more to the matter. Had Jesus accepted this offer, our salvation would have been impossible. In giving up the cross, Jesus would have sinned by worshipping Satan and therefore could not have been the spotless Lamb of God. He would also have failed to fulfill what the prophets said about the Messiah: suffering was to precede glory. By accepting Satan's "gift," there would be no crucifixion, no bloodshed, and no forgiveness of sins.

Jesus declined. He quoted from the book of Deuteronomy, where Moses gave the Law to the people—worship God and God alone (5:7). Again, the Israelites failed miserably, but again Jesus did not. He held true to the promise that God is in control.

I think it's easy to pass over this temptation. We automatically remind ourselves Jesus was God's Son and the plan had always been for him to suffer for our redemption. We forget that Jesus was also fully man. He knew that in just three short years, he would pay dearly for you and for me. Yet he stood on that mountaintop and refused to take the easy way out.

Have you ever been tempted to take an easier path than the one you believe would honor God? Perhaps you've cheated on a test, believing just this once it wouldn't matter. Perhaps you've lied on a business report or engaged in questionable practices, trying to tell yourself the end justified the means. Perhaps you're in a difficult marriage and find yourself drawn to someone else who brings out feelings you haven't had for a long time.

I know what it feels like to be tempted, to grab what seems right or necessary or take an easy way out of the hard work of being a follower of Christ. Most of us struggle with wanting to avoid pain. As I said, it's human nature to want what we can't always have—in this case an end to suffering, whether big or small.

And yet, in taking things into our own hands, we lose the opportunity to allow God to work on our behalf for the greater good.

A few nights ago, I participated in an online chat (if you don't know what that is, ask your kids!) on the subject of prayer. One woman wrote in to say she had been praying for a child who has been seriously ill for three years and yet God seems silent. Her temptation was to quit on God. Why bother praying when he doesn't answer?

In my mind's eye I could see her standing on top of that mountain with Satan whispering, "Forget God; he's forgotten you. Just worship me."

One of the hardest elements of our walk with God is to keep worshipping him even when it hurts. Jesus looked at everything Satan offered him, looked ahead to the cross and the agony, and chose to worship God.

giving in to charisma over character

The Greatest Show in Town

> Then he brought Him to Jerusalem, set Him on the pinnacle of the temple, and said to Him, "If You are the Son of God, throw Yourself down from here. For it is written:

'He shall give His angels charge over you,
To keep you,'
and, 'In their hands they shall bear you up,
Lest you dash your foot against a stone.'" (Luke 4:9–11)

In this final temptation, Satan took Jesus to the very pinnacle of the temple in Jerusalem, where in rabbinic tradition the Messiah would appear. It is likely that this was what is called the King's Gallery. The Jewish historian Josephus wrote, describing this pinnacle, that it "deserves to be mentioned among the most magnificent things under the sun: for upon a stupendous depth of a valley, scarcely to be fathomed by the eye of him that stands above, Herod erected a gallery of a vast height, from the top of which if any looked down, he would grow dizzy, his eyes not being able to reach so vast a depth."[2] The sight would be dizzying. There Satan tempted Christ to display his sonship.

Satan took two verses from Psalm 91 out of context and omitted an important phrase—Psalm 91:11 says, "He shall give His angels charge over you, to keep you *in all your ways*" (emphasis added). It is a telling omission. The Old Testament speaks many times about the "ways" of a righteous man or woman.

- "And now, Israel, what does the Lord your God require of you, but to fear the Lord your God, to walk in all His *ways*. . . ." (Deuteronomy 10:12; emphasis added)
- "For I have kept the *ways* of the Lord, / and have not wickedly departed from my God." (Psalm 18:21; emphasis added)
- "Blessed is every one who fears the Lord, / who walks in His *ways*." (Psalm 128:1; emphasis added)

Satan's cunning omission was an invitation to behave in a way a godly person would not—by desiring style over substance.

In essence, Satan was tempting Jesus to show off. His appeal was toward the spectacular—after all, what a sight it would be right there in the temple of Jerusalem for Christ to throw himself off the pinnacle! Everyone would see the rush of angel wings as they swooped in to rescue the Son of God.

But Jesus refused to test God. He knew that at any moment God might choose to deliver a sign (just as he had at the Jordan River, recorded in Matthew 3:16), but Christ would not ask for one. The children of Israel had demanded sign after sign in the desert, yet the miracles made no difference whatsoever. After each response from God, they still slipped back into their wrongful ways. Jesus refused to give in to the self-indulgent desire to have God respond to risky behavior; instead, he kept his life under the shadow of his Father's wings.

Jesus knew: Miracles don't change hearts. Obedience does.

I wonder how that sits with you? It can be hard, I know. We so often want miracles—something that will overwhelm and amaze us. We might have right desires at the root of things, but we're blinded by the methods.

God has given us his Holy Spirit to guide and direct us. He has given us his Word to be a light to our daily path. He has given us the body of Christ so that together we can work out our salvation with fear and trembling. But so often we want more. We want the feel-good moments when God shows up like a magician and pulls miracles out of a hat.

I would say to you that if you want to feel special, take a good, long look at the cross. There has never been a greater statement made by God than the sight of his Son stretched out on the gallows out of love for you and for me.

will she stand or will she fall?

Satan can and will tempt and test us in many ways. What he does not know is how we will respond. Like the little girl at the birthday party, will we grab the discarded piece of cake simply because we've been told not to? Will we pitch a fit, like the child in the store when we don't get what we want when we want it? Satan doesn't know.

We can give in. We can want what we don't have. We can want the glory without the suffering. Or we can look to Jesus, who gave us the perfect responses in his encounters with Satan:

- "God is my provider."
- "I will not take the easy way out."
- "I will not seek the spectacular; I will seek God's face."

I don't know what situations you are facing right now, but I know that Christ our Savior has left his footprints in the desert sand for us to follow. What Satan tempts us with is never what we are really longing for. It may appear to meet a need at the moment, but it will just take us deeper and deeper into the wilderness. Christ's steps keep us close to the heart of God.

deliverance discovered

1. In what areas of your life are you most tempted? Is it to grasp hold of what you feel you need now, to take an easy path out of a difficult place, or to rash and reckless behavior?
2. What is the strongest temptation you deal with?
3. What are some of the moments in your life when you have been tempted to take the easy way out?
4. In what places in your life or the life of your family does it seem that you might have compromised?

a prayer of deliverance

Father God,

I thank you that you led your own Son into the wilderness to be tested so that I can learn to be an overcomer.

I confess there are times in my life when I want to grasp hold of what I want, whether it is in your will for me or not. Forgive me, Father.

I confess that at times I long for an easier path than the one you have chosen for me. Forgive me, Father.

I confess that I have allowed some areas of my life to be shaped by this world and not by your heart. Forgive me, Father.

Teach me by your great grace to be more like Jesus. In his name I pray, amen.

EIGHT

let go and live in Christ's victory

The triumphant Christian does not fight for victory; he celebrates a victory already won. The victorious life is Christ's business, not yours.

—Reginald Wallis

The first step on the way to victory is to recognize the enemy.

—Corrie ten Boom

I know how to live on almost nothing or with everything. I have learned the secret of living in every situation, whether it is with a full stomach or empty, with plenty or little. For I can do everything with the help of Christ who gives me strength I need.

—Philippians 4:12–13 NLT

Don't let evil get the best of you; get the best of evil by doing good.

—Romans 12:21 MSG

So here's what I want you to do, God helping you: Take your everyday, ordinary life—your sleeping, eating, going-to-work, and walking-around life—and place it before God as an offering. Embracing what God does for you is the best thing you can do for him.

—Romans 12:1 msg

"It's not that I don't like Angela," she began, "I do. It's just that she can be a little . . . well, a bit of a goody-two-shoes, if you know what I mean."

"Oh, I do," her friend replied, putting her coffee cup down on the kitchen table. "She is always volunteering for everything—which is fine, obviously. But at times I question her motives."

"Yes, and that smile," the first woman added. "No one can be as happy as that all the time."

"Particularly married to her husband!" the second added with a laugh.

"Do you think they're happy?"

"I can't imagine how. Yet she's always so kind to him whenever they are together," the friend observed.

"That has to be an act, don't you think?"

"An act I'm sure my husband wouldn't object to my copying!"

The doorbell rang, and the woman went to see who it could possibly be.

"Who was it?" her friend asked when she returned.

"It's flowers," she said. "They're for me. Let's see who my secret admirer is!"

Thinking of you.
Angela

The fragrance of the flowers filled every corner of the room.

placing your life before God

In Romans 12:1, the apostle Paul told us, "Take your everyday, ordinary life—your sleeping, eating, going-to-work, and walking-around life—and place it before God as an offering" (MSG). For years I struggled with what placing my life before God would look like. How was I to place the everyday details of my life before him? Was it just a matter of prayer, or was there more involved? If the promise of God's strength in my weakness to overcome temptation rested in my surrendering everything I was to him, how did I do that?

To help answer that I'd like to take you back to 1980 and a British summer youth camp called Spring Harvest. More than two thousand young people gathered at a small town in Wales called Prestatyn. I was there as part of the worship team, and the main speaker was an Argentinean evangelist named Luis Palau. He spoke with great passion and intensity, which captivated me as a young, fervent believer. I had gone to church most of my life, but I wanted more than that. I wanted to know what God wanted me to do. I wanted to fulfill my destiny and know my life made a difference. I wanted to live like a follower of Christ and not just talk about it.

On the final night of the weeklong camp, Luis spoke on Christ's invitation recorded in Matthew's gospel: "If anyone desires to come after Me, let him deny himself, and take up his cross, and follow Me. For whoever desires to save his life will lose it, but whoever loses his life for My sake will find it" (16:24–25).

I had known that text since I was a child, but it never made any sense to me. How did one carry a cross?

At the time, I wondered if the evangelist Arthur Blessitt was the only one who "got it." Beginning on Christmas Day 1969, he had been carrying a twelve-foot cross around the world speaking of the love of Christ everywhere he went. When I was sixteen, I went with my youth group to hear him speak. It was an inspiring message—so much so that when we got back to our little town, one of our group, George, made a cross similar to the one Arthur had and began dragging it everywhere he went. That lasted for a few weeks until he turned too quickly during one of our "faith marches" along the beach and whacked my best friend, Andree, over the head with it. What began as a "march of faith" almost ended in a fistfight! After that, our minister suggested George might want to keep the cross at home from now on.

Honestly, though, I was confused. If God wanted us all to carry physical crosses, then I was ready and the kitchen table had better watch out. But it didn't make sense to me. We couldn't all do that—the world would be filled with people with sore heads and nowhere to eat lunch.

Then I heard Luis speak, and for the first time I began to understand. Luis spoke about the dichotomy between the Word of God and our will and emotions. He said that often they are at war. His remedy sounded simple. He said that every time my will was at odds with the revealed will of God, then taking up my cross every day simply meant dragging my will back in line with the will of God and placing my life under his protective care again.

Okay, so now that made sense to me. But in the months and years that followed, I made an interesting discovery about myself: at times it would have been far easier for me to drag a wooden cross around the world than to drag my will in line with the will of God. Fulfilling the demands of a task is fairly straightforward, but overcoming bad habits or selfish behaviors that have been indulged for years is a more challenging exercise.

What about you? We all struggle in different ways. Our will—and tucked right underneath that, our fear—make it hard to claim victory in certain areas of life. We wrestle with what we know to be true, we struggle to accept God's will, and we argue we know what's best. In other words, we're completely enslaved to our own desires. We'd rather drag that cross to Timbuktu and back rather than relinquish control of our lives.

At best, that is foolish and, at worst, deliberately sinful. Christ paid with everything he had so that you and I could be delivered from the things that hold us captive. So why do we choose to hang on to them?

Perhaps because they are so familiar or comforting, or perhaps because we're weak. Corrie ten Boom wrote that the first step to victory is to recognize the enemy,[1] but so often we are our own worst enemies. If left to our own devices, we can pretty much guarantee we'll fall over our best intentions time after time. Thankfully, although we will be tempted and tested in many ways in this life, if we can learn that when we pull our wills in line with his, God will teach us how to overcome in every area.

how Jesus overcame

The Greek word used in Luke 4 (where Satan tempted Jesus) for "temptation" is *peirasmos*. It simply means testing. The Word of God distinguishes between three kinds of testing: Satan tempts people, people can test God, and God tests his people.

Let's take a quick look at each of these and see how the Word of God directs our path to overcoming temptation. In identifying the avenues of temptation, we can see God's arsenal of weapons Christ used to be an overcomer.

Satan Tempts People

Paul wrote to the church in Thessalonica, "That's why I couldn't quit worrying; I had to know for myself how you were doing in the faith. I didn't want the Tempter getting to you and tearing down everything we had built up together" (1 Thessalonians 3:5 MSG).

God never tempts us or sets a trap to see if we will be faithful. In the book of James, we read, "Don't let anyone under pressure to give in to evil say, 'God is trying to trip me up.' God is impervious to evil, and puts evil in no one's way" (1:13 MSG). Yet how many times have you heard people accuse God when disaster strikes? How many times have you fallen prey to that excuse yourself?

God is never the author of evil. Satan is. But Satan's goal is to make you forget that point. When we are alert in our minds to the truth that Satan is the one whose carnivorous smile lies behind the evil he carefully places on our paths, it will be far easier to resist and overcome.

People Can Tempt or Test God

This happened over and over in the Old Testament record, as God's people demanded a sign God was still with them. It is tempting to want to do that. I can think of many moments in my life when I wanted God to give me some sign that he heard my prayers or that he was aware of what was going on in my life. Perhaps you have tried the old "open your Bible at random and stick your finger on a verse" routine too.

As I think back on those moments in my life when I doubted, I see them now as a lack of trust—and, even more, a lack of belief that I am totally loved by God.

Perhaps that is one of Satan's greatest tricks: to make us question the love of God. I can think of few things more injurious to God our Father than to doubt his love for us. What more could he have done to show us? It is one thing as a new believer to ask God for a sign, but as we grow and mature in our faith, one of the hallmarks is trust. We can be overwhelmed and overcome by doubt and fear, or by faith we can stand on what we know to be true and overcome fear with faith.

God Tests His People

One of the most profound passages in the book of the Law is found in Deuteronomy 8:

> Remember every road that God led you on for those forty years in the wilderness, pushing you to your limits, testing you so that he would know what you were made of, whether you would keep his commandments or not. He put you through hard times. He made you go hungry. Then he fed you with manna, something neither you nor your parents knew anything about, so you would learn that men and women don't live by bread only; we live by every word that comes from God's mouth. Your clothes didn't wear out and your feet didn't blister those forty years. You learned deep in your heart that God disciplines you in the same ways a father disciplines his child. (vv. 2–5 MSG)

The Israelites were tested many times during this period in their history. First, they were enslaved by the Egyptians. Then, after Pharaoh finally let them go a "mere" 430 years after they were taken into captivity, he changed his mind and sent soldiers to attack God's people. They must have been so frightened when they saw the chariots bearing down upon them.

And finally, because of their choices, they were lost in the desert for forty years, pushed to the limits of their ability, and crying out to God for answers, wondering if they'd made the wrong decision to leave Egypt.

Why were they put through so much? To learn the heart of their God. To understand that they were loved and treasured. To learn—to appreciate and accept the need to put their complete faith in God. And to see how capable they really were when they did put their faith in him. I believe that one of the most powerful fruits of testing is to begin to finally grasp that although we are weak, in Christ's strength, we are strong. Each time we are tested and by God's grace we stand, we grow in our knowledge of him and in our confidence that, indeed, "I can do all things through Christ who strengthens me" (Philippians 4:13).

So in looking at the three types of temptation, we immediately see the futility of the first two. When Satan tests us, or when we try to test God, it serves no purpose. But when God tests us, the testing is for *us*—to show us what is in us. (He obviously doesn't need to know what's in himself.) I know his heart well enough to understand he doesn't test us to shame us. I believe it has to be a gift of love—his own divine show-and-tell. He's showing us we're strong . . . in him. He's telling us it's okay to put down that cross and relinquish ourselves to him.

Is that a scary thought to you? For years I dragged my cross through life because I was afraid that if I gave it up, two things might happen. First, I was afraid if I stopped trying so hard to be a "good" Christian, then the enemy might overtake me. I knew he sets traps for God's children, and in my flawed reasoning I thought the harder I worked, the harder it would be to trip me up. Second, I was afraid if I stopped working so hard, I would see that there was very little in me for God to love.

It has taken me many years to understand that God simply wants us to embrace what he has already done for us and rest in that. What I discovered is that when I am trying so hard to live a good life, all the focus is on me. Then all I can see is where I am flawed or failing. When I take my eyes off myself and my performance, and focus instead on the love of God and the companionship of Christ, not only is there amazing joy in that place but peace too. Jesus wants us to live in his victory. He has already overcome the enemy. He has already paid for our sin.

When I was a young girl, I dropped a china plate that had sentimental value for my mom. I was horrified. At first I tried to hide all the pieces, but I felt so miserably guilty that I had to tell her. She looked at the pieces to see if the plate could be mended, but it had been irreparably shattered; so she threw the pieces away. Later that day I retrieved the pieces from the trash, determined to fix my mom's plate. I sat for a few frustrating hours trying to glue it back together to no avail. Mom heard me crying in my room, and when she saw what I was doing she said, "Sheila, I have already forgiven you for knocking the plate over. It's over and done with. Just let it go."

Resting in the love of God means letting go of all the broken pieces we cling to and clinging instead to him. An overcomer is not someone who has never fallen, but rather someone who knows where her true strength lies.

what would keep an overcomer from overcoming?

As we reflect on the three temptations Satan presented in such attractive packages to Jesus, fear is used as the bow to tie them all together. When we look at the first temptation, we see that Jesus was literally beginning to starve, so Satan played to that. He reminded Jesus he was hungry. He tried to make him look at what he didn't have.

Do you see how Satan uses fear to tempt us away from trust?

- *Look at your bank balance. You're not going to make it this month.*

- *Look at how exhausted you are. You don't have the energy to do what you need to do.*
- *You've splurged again and ruined your diet. You may as well quit.*
- *Do you see your child walking away from faith? She'll never come back. You blew it.*

All the while the deadly whisper is, *Look at how weak you are. What makes you think that you will ever succeed?*

Jesus' short and powerful reply was to point us back to the Word of God to counter what might seem true at the moment with what is *always* true.

> Don't fret or worry. Instead of worrying, pray. Let petitions and praises shape your worries into prayers, letting God know your concerns. Before you know it, a sense of God's wholeness, everything coming together for good, will come and settle you down. It's wonderful what happens when Christ displaces worry at the center of your life. (Philippians 4:6–7 MSG)

I love the phrase "when Christ displaces worry at the center of your life." That is how Jesus resisted temptation, and so can we.

Then Satan moved on to his second temptation—suggesting to Jesus there is an easy way out of pain. I think it will be interesting when we get to heaven to see how we'll view pain and suffering down here. I am not for a moment attempting to minimize the agony so many of us have to walk through during our lives. I have talked with parents who lost their children. I have visited women in prison whose lives were decimated by the cruelty of others. I have met a woman who is not able to have children naturally because her pelvis was crushed while being raped by her father when she was a child.

Yes, evil is very real. But it is no match for the love of God. Even when we are called to walk down a path we would never have chosen, I believe God is in the redeeming business. Nothing we have faced will be lost, and nothing we have lost will be lost forever. Just as Satan loves to show us our needs, he loves to play on our fears. But Jesus said his grace would be enough. There is nothing you or I will face today or tomorrow that we will face alone. Jesus will be there with us with everything we need to walk through it.

Think of the apostle Paul. In his second letter to the church in Corinth, he told them that he had what he described as "a thorn in the flesh" (2 Corinthians 12:7). He asked God three times to remove it, and God said no. But hear Paul's words as he responded to that answer:

> Satan's angel did his best to get me down; what he in fact did was push me to my knees. No danger then of walking around high and mighty! At first I didn't think of it as a gift, and begged God to remove it. Three times I did that, and then he told me, "My grace is enough; it's all you need. My strength comes into its own in your weakness." Once I heard that, I was glad to let it happen. I quit focusing on the handicap and began appreciating the gift. (vv. 7–9 MSG)

Finally, Satan tempted Jesus with showing off. He played on the fear of feeling insignificant in God's grand scheme.

Do you ever feel like a nobody? Do you wonder if anyone sees all that you do, or if anyone cares? Do you ever fear your voice will simply never be heard? Our culture and at times our churches seem more impressed with charisma than character. You see it on the news every day. We make heroes out of very flawed people and then wonder why they come crashing to the ground.

It has always been one of Satan's most powerful tools to tempt us to try to be "somebody." In the garden of Eden, that was his approach with Eve: "God knows that the moment you eat from that tree, you'll see what's really going on. You'll be just like God" (Genesis 3:4 MSG). The appeal was too much for Eve to resist, so she took from the only tree in the garden forbidden to her.

To Jesus on the top of the temple, Satan's approach was the same: *Show your stuff! Show them who you really are!* Perhaps Satan hoped Christ would plunge to his death.

How many times has Satan tripped us up by tempting us to grab it all? Power is a heady drug. Satan's whisper is, *You'll get away with it.* But Jesus said, "It is written again, 'You shall not tempt the LORD your God'" (Matthew 4:7). It is to God, and God alone, that all glory goes. We are to enjoy his provision.

We need not fear anything. God has shown us again and again that he has our best interests at heart. He will provide for us. He will comfort us. He will reveal himself to us.

the joy of servanthood

For the last twelve years I have traveled for about thirty weekends every year with a team of women called Women of Faith. The core team has changed a little of late. We lost our beloved Barbara Johnson in July 2007 to brain cancer, and at the beginning of 2008 Thelma Wells moved on to other speaking and television appearances. But for ten years we were all together.

One of the greatest lessons God taught me through those years is the joy of serving those you walk and work beside. *Beside,* not *in front of.* There is something in our human flesh that doesn't want to be compared with others, but if we have to we would like to come out on top. One of heaven's most liberating secrets is to pray for the success of those around you. Satan hates it when we refuse to fall for his theatrics. But I have discovered that it's hard to fall off a pedestal when you are washing someone's feet.

Jesus showed his friends that the math of the new kingdom offered a whole new way to live.

> When he was safe at home, he asked them, "What were you discussing on the road?" The silence was deafening—they had been arguing with one another over who among them was greatest. He sat down and summoned the Twelve. "So you want first place? Then take the last place. Be the servant of all." (Mark 9:33–35 MSG)

One of the greatest advantages of putting down that self-made cross we drag through life is that it frees up our hands. It frees us to worship our Father. It frees us to wash our sisters' feet. It frees us to walk beside each other without whacking each other over the head and getting splinters in our hair! It frees us to be like Jesus.

The longer I am in relationship with Jesus, the simpler life seems. Notice that I said *simpler,* not *easier*. When I think back to my teen years and my confusion over "taking up my cross," I see now that being an overcomer in Christ is simply doing the things Jesus did. The great news in the midst of it is that what gave Jesus strength to resist the enemy, the internal struggle, or the lack of understanding in others was the Word of God and the fellowship of his Father. We struggle so hard to get it right, but Jesus said, "Just follow me and do what I do!"

deliverance discovered

1. In what areas of your life are you being invited to pull your will in line with the will of God?
2. In what areas is it hard for you to trust God? Why do you think that is?
3. Where do you feel as if you are just dragging your cross through life?
4. In what new ways could you serve those in your life?

a prayer of deliverance

Father God,

I thank you that there is no temptation I will face that Christ has not faced before me. I acknowledge before you that at times fear, not faith, makes my choices for me—and that I'm often left dragging a very heavy cross because of it. Help me to replace fear with Christ at the center of my life. Help me to recognize and resist the lies of the enemy. Thank you that you love me right now just as I am and that overcomers serve best on their knees.

In Jesus' name, amen.

NINE
shame on you!

The purpose of being guilty is to bring us to Jesus. Once we are there, then its purpose is finished. If we continue to make ourselves guilty—to blame ourselves—then that is sin in itself.

—Corrie ten Boom

There smites nothing so sharp, nor smelleth so sour as shame.

—William Langland

A pervasive sense of shame is the ongoing premise that one is fundamentally bad, inadequate, defective, unworthy, or not fully valid as a human being.

—Merle Fossum

The religion scholars and Pharisees led in a woman who had been caught in an act of adultery. They stood her in plain sight of everyone and said, "Teacher, this woman was caught red-handed in the act of adultery."

—John 8:3–4 MSG

When the Pharisee who had invited him saw this, he said to himself, "If this man was the prophet I thought he was, he would have known what kind of woman this is who is falling all over him."

—Luke 7:39 MSG

She didn't drive, and since no one had offered to pick her up, she took the bus. She had been surprised by the invitation to join the office crowd for dinner. They were kind to her at work, but it was clear she didn't really fit in. As she reflected back on the invitation, she wondered if they felt obliged to include her. After all, she had walked into the lunchroom when they were discussing their plans for the following evening.

"Oh, Eva, we were just talking about a little dinner party we're going to have tomorrow night. It's nothing fancy, but we'd love it if you came," one said.

At first she felt elated. Perhaps this was the open door she had been praying for. But as she sat on the bus, she second-guessed herself and began to feel like a fool.

"Why didn't I just say I had plans?" she asked herself as her frustration and anxiety level grew.

The rain was beginning to fall as she got off the bus. This stop was the closest to the Millers' home, but it was still a five-minute walk. As the bus pulled away, the back tire ran through a huge puddle and splashed muddy water all over her shoes and coat. She pulled a scarf over her head and hurried down the street.

As she arrived, she could hear music coming from the front room of the house. She stopped and looked in the bay window at the crowd gathered inside. They all looked as if they belonged. They were laughing and talking, and in that moment Eva knew she could not go in. She *didn't* belong.

She pulled the scarf down lower on her forehead and hurried off into the rain.

bad shame versus good guilt

Cheap perfume. That's how shame feels to me. It's like the cheap, cloying perfume I used to get as a child at Christmastime. Mine came in a little bottle in the shape of a dog, which I loved, but the fragrance inside was terrible. One Christmas, as I opened the container and sniffed, hoping this year the manufacturer had come up with something more pleasant-smelling, my little brother ran past me with his new robot. He rammed into me at full throttle and the whole bottle poured out onto my sweater. The smell was atrocious! I took my sweater off, took a bath, and then I took another bath. But I smelled of that cheap perfume until Easter!

Shame is nauseating. It is heavy. Lewis Smedes, in his wonderful book *Shame and Grace,* described it as "a dead weight of not-good-enough-ness."[1] It is like a ravenous, demanding monster, and no matter how much you feed it to quiet the noise, it is never enough. It sits in the pit of your stomach or wraps its cold arms around your shoulders. And it doesn't let go.

Guilt is something different. Guilt has a purpose. It is there to (hopefully) teach you, and it has a point of beginning and ending. Shame is not as clearly defined as guilt. It doesn't seem to have a beginning or an end; it just is.

Guilt tells me I have done something wrong. With that awareness there is hope. I can go to the person I have hurt and ask him or her to forgive me. Or I can work to right an injustice I committed.

Shame, on the other hand, tells me I *am* something wrong. There is no hope there. Where do I go to change who I am at my core? How can I fix it?

My son is almost twelve now, and I have found it an interesting study to observe how he responds to life. If Christian has done something wrong, he has a very appropriate sense of guilt.

Barry asked me before the Women of Faith 2008 conference

schedule began if I thought it might be fun for Christian to record a rap video of one of his favorite Christian songs that we could show to our audience. I loved the idea. Christian traveled with me from six weeks of age until he was eight, and our audience often asked how he was doing and what he looked like now.

Barry has a background in television, so he was able to produce a video of Christian in our garage with the help of one of our friends, Dave Koss. At the end of the shoot, we had large rolls of paper and spray paint left over (it was a lively video!), so Barry told Christian he could go into the yard and paint the paper any way he wanted. Later that evening Barry took our dogs out into the yard and became aware of a change in our scenery. Our magnolia tree was now pink in places. Part of our fence was blue. And written on the side of our house in letters large enough to see in Scotland was a short but pithy "HI!" Barry just about choked.

When he asked Christian about it, our son froze. He finally muttered a few words about being overcome by fumes and having no memory of the event. Barry suggested he go up to his room and see if quiet reflection would help his memory.

When Christian finally came down, he was very contrite. With big tears running down his face he told his dad and me that he understood our disappointment at his actions and at how the yard now looked, and that he would pay for paint remover from his allowance and spend a day tidying up the whole yard. And he did—including removing the pink paint from every magnolia leaf!

I was very grateful to see that kind of remorse in my son's heart. He had moved from something he had been caught at to how his actions had affected us. That is good guilt, not shame.

Shame is a devastating sickness of the soul. It tells us not to show up. It tells us we don't belong. It tells us that if people knew who we really are, we would be asked to leave. Shame doesn't even have to make sense because it weighs so much and takes up so much space in our lives we don't even think to stop and question its right to be there. Guilt would have been the appropriate response of Adam and Eve to their tragic disobedience in the garden of Eden, but shame was the hellish breath the serpent covered them with. Guilt can be a door, whereas shame is a dead end.

But worst of all, shame offers no hope.

desperate enough to try

The gospel of Mark gives us an account of a woman who clung to hope even as others heaped shame upon her.

> A woman who had suffered a condition of hemorrhaging for twelve years—a long succession of physicians had treated her, and treated her badly, taking all her money and leaving her worse off than before—had heard about Jesus. (5:25–26 MSG)

It is difficult for us today to understand what this condition meant to a woman in her culture. Most theologians agree that her condition was most likely a bleeding uterus. This would have made her "unclean." The ramifications of such ceremonial uncleanliness were huge to a Jewish woman, who would become a literal outcast.

> If a woman has a discharge of blood for many days, but not at the time of her monthly period, or has a discharge that continues beyond the time of her period, she is unclean the same as during the time of her period. Every bed on which she lies during the time of the discharge and everything on which she sits becomes unclean the same as in her monthly period. Anyone who touches these things becomes unclean. (Leviticus 15:25–27 MSG)

This woman had no life. In her desperation, she had spent every cent she had trying to find a cure. Not only wasn't she better, she was broke and her condition was worse. She was desperate. She had heard of a man who was healing people, and I can imagine she thought this was her last chance.

There was a common superstition in her day that the power of a person was transferred to their clothes, so she believed if she could just touch the edge of Jesus' garments she would be healed. What made that so appealing, too, is that the healing could be anonymous. She could slip in, touch his robe, and disappear once more into the crowd. Shame told her she did not belong, but she was desperate for hope.

Jesus had arrived in town. She heard the noise as she cowered in a quiet alley. It wasn't the noise of an angry rabble or the noise when the Roman soldiers rode through town; it was the sound of hope. She waited for the crowd to pass, and then she forced herself to take a few steps toward them. Her mind was racing.

What if someone sees me?

What if I am recognized?

Or, worst of all, *What if I touch him and nothing happens? How will I go on living then?*

She knew she had to try. How could her life be any worse than it was right now?

She was soul-sick with loneliness and despair. Keeping her head down, she approached the crowd. It was dense. People were pushing to get a better view of Jesus, to get closer to him. Ironically, it was her very shame that made way for her. Bent over as she was, one or two people turned to see what was behind them and cleared enough of a path for her bone-weary arm to stretch out and touch the edge of Jesus' robe.

Suddenly, in an instant, something happened. She felt it inside! It was as if someone had pulled open the drapes into the darkest place of her soul, and dazzling, healing light came flooding in. She didn't know whether to laugh or cry. She could hear laughter, but she could feel tears. It was true! *He is the Messiah and I touched him!* She thought of her family. She could hold them now. She could finally touch them and cook for them and look into their eyes.

Just as she turned to slip out of the crowd, something happened. Jesus was used to being surrounded by the pushing crowds, but he knew something else had taken place. He had felt healing power leave his body. So he asked, "Who touched me?" The disciples thought the question ridiculous—after all, he was surrounded by people pushing and shoving—but Jesus patiently waited for an answer.

The woman didn't have to do anything; Jesus would have let her disappear into the crowd. But he gave her a moment to speak up. He gave her a chance to be healed at a deeper level. She had been cleansed of her physical ailment, but she needed to let go of her shame.

It must have taken every bit of courage within the woman to come forward, but she did. She told Jesus the whole story. Jesus said to her, "Daughter, your faith has healed you. Go in peace" (Mark 5:34 NIV). This is the only time Jesus addressed a woman as "daughter" in all four Gospels. I am sure his tender and inclusive words dispelled shame as quickly as the morning sun dispels an early mist.

letting go

As I reread this woman's story and imagined what it must have been like that day, I began to see you and me standing beside her. Our issues are different, but our needs are the same. One of the scariest things to do on this earth is to voice that we have a problem.

Shame tells us to keep the secret, but then who is holding the keys to our prison? When we decide that it is time to tell, we find that the keys have been in our hands all along.

Not only did this woman reach out, but she reached out to Jesus. There are many places in our culture where the shame-filled are invited to go, but only Jesus has the power to heal. Perhaps the most liberating part of her story for us is that she told Jesus the whole truth. She told her story and wasn't consumed by it. She left us a path.

She Took a Risk

This woman took the first crucial step of just *doing* something. This is perhaps the most difficult part of all. Taking a risk requires first admitting you have a problem. With shame that is hard, because shame tells you not to ever take a risk again.

It all depends on how desperate you are. Someone once told me when the pain of staying the same became greater than the pain of change, then I'd be ready to change. I reached that point in my life in 1992. I didn't honestly know what was wrong with me, but I knew I was miserable and tired of living. If I had been able to identify a sin I had committed or was involved in, then I could have confessed it. But that wasn't the issue. The issue was that at my very core I felt "bad."

Does that ring true to you as well? Do you live with a familiar sense of not being good enough? Shame keeps us isolated. We don't speak up because, well, who are we to say anything? We don't feel free to pray in a group because we are sure that at some level others are judging us.

Things could have gone very differently for the woman in the crowd that day. What if she had made it right to where Jesus was standing and at the last moment succumbed to the internal voices that told her she had no right to even show her face in public? She might have lived for the rest of her life wondering if that was her moment and she had missed it.

She Reached Out to Jesus

This woman heard there was someone who was healing people and that his name was Jesus. She went to the only one who seemed to be able to change lives. Even though my own personal journey took me to a psychiatric hospital, where I received treatment for clinical depression and wonderful counseling, I knew my ultimate healing would be through Christ my Savior. He is the only one who can cure the sickness that is in our souls.

I love the fact that she went directly to Jesus. She didn't try to go to one of his friends and see if he would introduce her; she went directly to the healer himself. Sometimes we are more inclined to go to our friends before we go to the Father of our friends. I believe with all my heart in the beauty and strength of the body of Christ, but we must never forget that Christ is the head.

In Telling Her Story She Allowed Herself to Be Seen

I think this is the most beautiful part of this woman's journey. Jesus gave her a choice. She could have received her healing and disappeared once more into the crowd, but instead she chose to speak. She chose to tell Jesus her story and received an even greater blessing. When Jesus asked, "Who touched me?" she could have walked away unseen. She would have been physically healed but still sick at heart.

I will never forget the first time I told my story from the stage. I was terrified. To stand before a large crowd of Christian women and admit that the shame and despair in my life sent me to a "prison" before I could be set free went against everything I grew up believing. I gave my life to Jesus at eleven, but I kept my shame.

I believed if anyone knew what a worthless person I was, I would be exposed and shunned.

Believe it or not, I still struggle with this at times. Even though I am part of a team of wonderful women who love me and who are my friends, there are moments when the old beliefs float to the surface. Satan whispers,

- *You don't belong here.*
- *People don't really like you.*
- *Everyone can see there is something wrong with you.*

When this happens, I have to make an intentional choice to resist the lies of the enemy. I have to remember that although my childhood painted a lot of shame on my heart, as a woman of God I was given a blank canvas. The picture now coloring my innermost being is a beautiful thing. I may not be spared from the disappointments and frustrations we all face as adults, but I am changed. God whispers,

- *You are beautiful.*
- *You are loved.*
- *You are worth loving.*

Many of you look in the mirror and still see the scars of your youth, your pain, your shame. Messages from childhood are potent. If you were told as a child that you were fat or ugly, that you were a mistake or an inconvenience, you had no defenses to counter that. Children believe adults.

I have a friend who was sexually abused when she was just five years old. At five she was cute as a bug with lovely long hair and a bright smile. Unable to tell her parents what had happened because she felt so ashamed, she began to hide more and more. As the years passed, she used food to keep a formidable wall between herself and anyone who would try to harm her.

Sometimes she fought back. Knowing she needed to work on her physical self, she tried every diet in the book to get rid of the excess weight that years of overeating had given her. They all worked for a while, but they never lasted because food was not the core issue. It took her forty years, and the help of a good therapist, to understand that she was determined to never look pretty again because bad things happen to pretty girls. She had to learn to let go of all her shame. Today, thankfully, like the woman Jesus healed, she is free.

a father's love

One of the things I am very aware of not having in my life is the love of my father. He died when my sister, my brother, and I were under seven, so any memories I have of him are very sporadic or from photographs. My mom did a first-class job of loving us and providing a stable home and Christian environment for us to grow up in, but I know now that it is hard to make up that loss in the life of a daughter.

It's your dad who tells you that you are beautiful.

It's your dad who picks you up over his head and carries you on his shoulders.

It's your dad who will fight the monsters under your bed.

It's your dad who tells you that you are worth a lot, so don't settle for the first guy who tells you you're pretty.

Many young girls are growing up without a dad in their lives on a daily, consistent basis. The ideal scenario for those girls would be that those within the church community would stand in the gap. All too often, however, the church can be a place where shame is fed. I heard someone say that the hour or two (or three or four, depending on your denomination!) we spend worshipping on a Sunday is the time when we are the least honest and real. Perhaps that is because we are afraid to show who we really are in case we are rejected or judged.

I remember an incident as a teenager that left a mark on me for some time. Andree, my best friend, and I had spent Sunday afternoon on the beach talking to people about Jesus and inviting them to a youth service we were having the following Sunday. We realized as the sun began to go down that we didn't have time to get back to our own evening service, so we thought it might be fun to go to another church that was closer. We had had such a great day that we wanted to join in with other believers and thank God.

We got there just as the service was about to begin. We were standing at the back looking for a place to sit when one of the deacons came up to me and asked me to step outside. He explained that as we were wearing jeans we could not come into the service. With that, he closed the church door.

I thought about that incident for a long time. This man had no idea that my friend and I were very committed Christians. We might have been girls who were looking for God and this was our first attempt to attend a service. The message we received was clear: "You don't fit in here. You are not acceptable. Come back when you look 'right.'"

If you have been shamed by the church, my heart aches for you.

I wonder if the woman in the crowd that day received any looks that might have made her turn around? If she did, they didn't stop her. She took a risk and followed it all the way through.

the only way

The well of shame is deep. It might be your appearance that you are ashamed of, or a lack of education. It can be something as simple as feeling like you don't fit in well with a crowd. Whatever the source, shame is debilitating and isolating. Jesus invites us to come to him just as we are and touch the hem of his garment. He longs to heal us and set us free to tell our story.

I wonder how this woman's life affected those around her after her healing. She went from being someone who didn't even have the right to look another human being in the eye to one who had been personally touched and addressed by Jesus. The glorious thing about healing from the crushing weight of shame is the hope it can offer to others. Perhaps her one brave act of pushing through the crowd to touch Jesus became an invitation to others to do the same. When you have been set free, your life becomes an open door showing others the way.

deliverance discovered

1. Take some time to identify moments in your life when you have felt shamed.
2. What do the voices of shame tell you?
3. How does shame make you feel? Is it fear or disgust or loneliness?
4. Do you believe you are ready to change? How?

a prayer of deliverance

Father God,

When you created this world, you looked at it and said it was good. I know when you look down on me, you look on me, too, with love and delight; but at times it is hard for me to receive your love. Help me to identify the voices of shame and come to you for healing.

In Jesus' name I will take a risk. I will come to Jesus. I will tell my story out loud.

For Jesus' sake, amen.

TEN
shame on him

Christ redeemed us from that self-defeating, cursed life by absorbing it completely into himself. Do you remember the Scripture that says, "Cursed is everyone who hangs on a tree"? That is what happened when Jesus was nailed to the cross: He became a curse, and at the same time dissolved the curse.

—Galatians 3:13 msg

Alexander, Caesar, Charlemagne, and myself founded empires; but upon what did we rest the creations of our genius? Upon force. Jesus Christ alone founded his empire upon love, and at this hour millions of men would die for him.

—Napoleon Bonaparte

Assail'd by scandal and the tongue of strife,
His only answer was, a blameless life.

—William Cowper

Christ is God acting like God in the lowly raiments of human flesh.

—A. W. Tozer

He is despised and rejected by men,
A Man of sorrows and acquainted with grief.
And we hid, as it were, our faces from Him;
He was despised, and we did not esteem Him.
Surely He has borne our griefs and carried our sorrows;
Yet we esteemed Him stricken, smitten by God, and afflicted.
But He was wounded for our transgressions,
He *was* bruised for our iniquities;
The chastisement for our peace was upon Him,
And by His stripes we are healed.

—Isaiah 53:3–5

"Get up . . . now!" the voice yelled at him.

It was hard to see who it was at first with the light streaming into his cell, but he certainly knew the voice.

Roman scum, he thought.

"Move, now, before they change their minds," the guard said.

"It's not supposed to be today," he cried. "I have weeks yet. It's supposed to be them in the cell next door!"

"Get up!" was all the guard would say as he kicked the prisoner's legs. "Move out of here. Go."

"Go where?" he asked. "Am I being given another trial?"

"No," the guard said. "You are free to go."

"Free to go? What do you mean, 'free to go'?" he asked. "Is this your idea of a joke?"

"It's no joke," the guard said. "They asked for you."

The fresh air and sunlight hit his face as he stumbled up the stairs to freedom. He kept moving until the prison was out of sight. There was a crowd surging up the hill out of the city, so he decided to hide himself in a sea of bodies until he could work out where to go. They kept moving and shouting, but he kept his head down. Then they suddenly stopped and for a moment it was quiet. He looked up and saw that they were on the side of Golgotha and that rather than being executed, he was watching three other men face the end.

Someone touched his shoulder. As he turned in fear and suspicion, he recognized the man's face.

"What are you doing here, Barabbas?" he asked.

"I have no idea," he said.

paid in full

When I was a young girl, I had a recurring nightmare. In this terrible dream, I was about to be executed for a crime I didn't commit, but I couldn't get anyone to listen to me. There was a prison guard on each side, and they were taking me down a long corridor that had a closed door at the end. I knew when I reached that door I was to be executed.

We passed people I knew, but it was as if they couldn't hear me; they didn't even stop their conversations or turn toward me. I could feel my heart beat so fast I thought it would burst out of my chest.

Just before we got to the execution chamber, I would wake up in a cold sweat with tears pouring down my face. The dream was so real and vivid it always took me a few moments to convince myself it was just a nightmare and that I was actually safe in my bedroom with my sister fast asleep beside me.

Now when I think back on that nightmare, I know it had to do with my father's death and my feelings of confusion and responsibility. But I also know it's a perfect example of the reality Christ spared each one of us from. For those of us who love him and have been forgiven by him, he turned the nightmare that would have been ours into the gift of life. Most of us would not be guilty of crimes any human court might convict us of, but in the eyes of a holy God, we all stand condemned for the sin we were born into and the choices we have made. Jesus took the shame and judgment that was on us, and he heaped it upon himself.

It hurts me to think of the number of us who love Jesus but have spent years feeling shamed and unworthy when he already paid the ultimate price so we could be free and loved. That can change!

We can never fully plumb the depths of all Christ did for us on the cross, but there are three facets of his work in particular that I would like us to examine and celebrate.

The writer to the Hebrews talked about the imperfection of the Old Testament system of ritual cleansing and forgiveness using the body of a goat. Superseding this flawed provision, Christ became the perfect "scapegoat" (Hebrews 9:13–14). Under Old Testament judicial law, it was clear that anyone who was crucified or hung on a tree was cursed before God and man. Christ became that curse to free each one of us.

Perhaps the darkest moment of all was when Jesus cried out, "My God, My God, why have You forsaken Me?" (Matthew 27:46).

As we will discover, we are written into every scene.

the scapegoat

God cannot look on sin. Yet through all of history, his people have not kept themselves from sinning. In the Old Testament, God had to make a way to deal with the sins of the people. In Leviticus we read that a goat was chosen to carry the sins of the people out into the wilderness, symbolically removing the sin from them so that it couldn't be seen anymore.

> But the goat on which the lot fell to be the scapegoat shall be presented alive before the LORD, to make atonement upon it, and to let it go as the scapegoat into the wilderness. (16:10)

The priest would make atonement over the goat and symbolically transfer all of Israel's guilt to it. Then the goat would be taken out by one man into the wilderness and released when they were a long distance from Jerusalem. The man would then return and have to be ceremonially cleaned; he was considered contaminated by even being in the presence of the scapegoat.

It was an imperfect system that was later amended after one goat merrily returned to the people, which they took as a very bad sign! From that year on, the one who led the goat out for about six and a half miles was then instructed to push the goat over the side of the mountain to ensure that the sins of the people would not return to them.

Yet, as the writer to the Hebrews said,

> No matter how many sacrifices were offered year after year, they never added up to a complete solution. If they had, the worshipers would have gone merrily on their way, no longer dragged down by their sins. But instead of removing awareness of sin, when those animal sacrifices were repeated over and over they actually heightened awareness and guilt. The plain fact is that bull and goat blood can't get rid of sin. (10:2–4 MSG)

The New King James Version translates verse 4, "For it is not possible that the blood of bulls and goats could take away sins." The Greek word used for "not possible" is the strongest word that could be used—the same word used when Peter cut off the ear of the high priest's slave and it could not be replaced (Luke 22:50). In other words, the Israelites wanted to believe there was no way their sins could ever be revisited. Yet the very fact that the scapegoat ritual had to be repeated over and over each year shows how ineffective the system was. If the people had been really cleansed, there would have been no need to repeat the ceremony.

Only Jesus could make a one-time sacrifice and totally remove our sins so that we no longer carry them.

When the enemy torments you about some past, confessed sin, remember you no longer live under the old system where any old goat could drag it back to your door. What Jesus did on the cross was complete and total, and you don't have to deal with it. Your sin has been cut off—gone as far as the east is from the west—and God chooses to remember it no more (Psalm 103:12). That is good news!

If you find it hard to let the impact of that good news sink right to the depth of your heart and soul, try this: one thing I have found helpful from time to time when I have felt burdened by a past failure or persistent flaw is to write it down on a piece of paper, examine it, bring it before the Lord, and then burn it.

Let me give you an example. I used to have a problem with saying that I had done things I hadn't done or listened to CDs I hadn't listened to or seen movies that I hadn't seen because I wanted to "go with the flow." I would hear myself do it and think, *This is ridiculous. Why did I just say that I saw that movie when I didn't?* It was only when I recognized and owned this as sin that I could deal with it. So I wrote out on a piece of paper,

> Father,
>
> Sometimes I say things that aren't true because I want people to like me. I know that this is wrong and ask you to forgive me.

Then I lit the piece of paper and threw it in the fireplace. As it burned, I thanked my Father for his grace that covers my sin. As

I watched the burning paper turn to ashes, I knew that with God's help, I would never have to go back there again.

he became a curse for us

We live in a culture where very little respect is given to the human body. Modesty appears to be a thing of the past. I find it heart-breaking to see the way young girls dress, as if they have no sense of how special they are, how treasured they are by God. That was not the way things were in Jesus' time. The body was regarded as sacred, so there could be no greater affront than to have a body exposed to public view in death by hanging.

Hanging was the most extreme form of desecration and humiliation possible. When someone was publicly crucified, it said to everyone that this person was under the curse of God. The Jewish people believed that this curse was so strong that to leave the body up for more than a day would infect and symbolically curse their very own land.

> If a man has committed a sin deserving of death, and he is put to death, and you hang him on a tree, his body shall not remain overnight on the tree, but you shall surely bury him that day, so that you do not defile the land which the Lord your God is giving you as an inheritance; for he who is hanged is accursed of God. (Deuteronomy 21:22–23)

One of Christian's favorite Bible stories when he was a little boy was the story of the battle of Jericho. The idea that he could march round a city seven times, blow his horn, and the walls would come down seemed extremely appealing. It was therefore a great disappointment to him when he recruited several of his friends and tried this strategy on his kindergarten class to no avail.

After the defeat of Jericho, Joshua and the people of Israel moved on to take the city of Ai. Joshua chose thirty thousand men to fight the men of Ai. God blessed his battle strategy and the whole city was taken. All the men were slaughtered by the sword . . . except for the king of Ai. The king was brought to Joshua and, as a sign of God's contempt, was hung on a tree, open to public contempt.

This act was intended to strike fear into leaders of other tribes and cities when the news reached them of what had happened. But even then, as much as Joshua desired to send a message to his enemies, by nightfall the king's body was taken down and buried at the gate under a pile of stones. God's people respected the severity of public hanging but would not leave the body up for more than a few hours, because the curse was so potent.

Crucifixion was the most humiliating way Christ could have offered to take our sin upon himself. We will never be able to fully realize what Christ did for us. Not only was he in physical and spiritual pain on the cross, but he took on a place of public degradation, dying under the curse of his own Father out of his love for you and me.

In Roman law, crucifixion was reserved for the lowest classes and worst criminals. No Roman citizen could be executed this way without a direct edict from Caesar. Not only that, but it is rare to even find evidence of crucifixion because the bodies were usually pulled off the cross and thrown on a trash pile to be devoured by animals. Yet God chose crucifixion for his Son.

Christ's life exemplified the extreme measures God took for us. Jesus didn't have to be born into such poverty. He could have been born into a comfortable middle-class home. He could have died by stoning, as Stephen did in the book of Acts, which was a form of execution more favored by the Jews. Instead, Jesus chose the most humble beginning and the most humiliating end.

Such love is hard to fathom. Such love tells you there was no length too great for the Father to go to out of love for you. Such love should tell our shame to be gone in Jesus' name.

the cry of desolation

Jesus became our scapegoat. He became the curse in our stead. And now he hung on the cross, mocked and ridiculed.

From noon until three o'clock that day, the sky became dark. The prophet Amos wrote of this happening: "'And it shall come to pass in that day,' says the Lord God, 'that I will make the sun go down at noon, and I will darken the earth in broad daylight'" (8:9).

In Amos, darkness was seen as a sign of God's judgment. This judgment was not on Christ; his judgment came at the hour of three o'clock. But for the three hours before that, the judgment of God was on the land and on the people who were brutalizing his Son. As Amos wrote, "I will make it like mourning for an only son" (8:10).

I wonder if Jesus felt the presence of his Father slowly seeping away from him during those hours. I can only imagine the heaviness in the air as God passed judgment on his people. To us it would be frightening enough, but to Jesus it must have felt as though a knife pierced through his heart.

Finally, at the ninth hour, Jesus cried out, "My God, My God, why have You forsaken Me?" (Matthew 27:46).

It is impossible for us to know the full sense of how the Father and Son were divided at that moment, because we are not told. All we can do is judge it against the close companionship we know Jesus had with his Father.

> All things have been delivered to Me by My Father, and no one knows the Son except the Father. Nor does anyone know the Father

> except the Son, and the one to whom the Son wills to reveal Him. (Matthew 11:27)

Jesus knew his Father was not there as he tasted the very essence of hell—separation from God. And yet in that moment was triumph, too, as Jesus once and for all took every sin, every ounce of shame and condemnation we will ever deserve, and embraced it. It was ordained that he would take our place under judgment, and with love he accepted that role.

Such is his love that he believed we were worth dying for.

I will never be able to wrap my mind around that truth, for it is beyond human understanding. But I have staked my life on it. Jesus believes I was worth it all. Jesus believes that you were worth every blow he took, every thorn that ripped into the delicate tissue in his head, and every strike of the hammer against the nails that pierced his wrists. You are loved and valued more than you could ever hope or ask for. The greatest love story that Hollywood ever thought up could not hold a candle to the flame that burns in God's heart for you, dear sister!

it is finished!

At the moment Christ let out his final cry on the cross, the veil in the temple was ripped from top to bottom (Matthew 27:51). No longer was there a need for a temple, for Jesus is the temple. No longer was there a need for a veil to hide the presence of God in the Holy of Holies, for Jesus is the place where you and I come face-to-face with God our Father.

Jesus took our shame on himself so you and I can come into our Father's presence, as a child would run into the arms of a papa who loves her. What more, dear sisters, needs to be said? It is finished! We are free!

As I reflect on what the death and sacrifice of Christ say to you and to me, I am overwhelmed. To be loved like this demands something in return. If God looked at our fragile, broken lives and determined that no price would be too high to salvage them, then I don't want to miss one moment of my destiny. I am tired of us looking at our reflections in the old mirror of what seems true to us. Instead, let's see ourselves in God's mirror.

deliverance discovered

1. Jesus has carried our shame so that we no longer have to carry it. We are free from the curse because he became a curse for us. How does that make you feel?
2. Do you feel forsaken? What would it look like to let Jesus take your sorrow and set you free?
3. Do you still hold on to some secret sin? What is it? We no longer need a scapegoat, for Jesus has carried our sins for us on the tree. Will you give your sin over to Jesus today?

a prayer of deliverance

Dear Father,

There are no words that could ever begin to thank you for what Jesus did for me. That he would willingly endure such agony and not cry out for help is more than I can understand. Father, how your heart must have wept over his pain and what my sin did to him.

I thank you that Jesus became shame so that I could live without shame. Help me to choose to live in that truth and remember that "it is finished!"

In Jesus' name, amen.

ELEVEN

you are you for a reason

The greatest burden we have to carry in life is self; the most difficult thing we have to manage is self.

—Hannah Whitall Smith

To be nobody but yourself—in a world that is doing its best, night and day, to make you everybody else—means to fight the hardest battle any human being can fight, and never stop fighting.

—E. E. Cummings

Rules for Self Discovery:

1. What we want most;
2. What we think about most;
3. How we use our money;
4. What we do with our leisure time;
5. The company we enjoy;
6. Who and what we admire;
7. What we laugh at.

—A. W. Tozer

After rising from the dead, Jesus appeared early on Sunday morning to Mary Magdalene, whom he had delivered from seven demons. She went to his former companions, now weeping and carrying on, and told them. When they heard her report that she had seen him alive and well, they didn't believe her.

—Mark 16:9–11 msg

Tell it to God—he's the one behind all this,
he's the one who dragged me into this mess.
Look at me—I shout "Murder!" and I'm ignored;
I call for help and no one bothers to stop.
God threw a barricade across my path—I'm stymied;
he turned out all the lights—I'm stuck in the dark.
He destroyed my reputation,
robbed me of all self-respect.
He tore me apart piece by piece—I'm ruined!

—Job 19:6–10 msg

It seemed to her that the voices were louder at night. Perhaps it was only that the world was quieter then and the voices had little competition. She dreaded the nights.

Sometimes the voices came together like a pack of hungry wolves looking to consume any sanity she still held on to. But tonight it was just one. Just one tormentor to encircle her with insults and malice. His breath was foul, like the stench that rose up from the garbage on the street below when the sun blazed in the sky.

"You will never be free," he began. "You are nothing but a miserable outcast. No one cares if you live or if you die. You are ours while you live, and you will be ours forever when you die." His laugh was like that of a madman.

She wondered why she had been born, for no one took any pleasure in her life, least of all the one whose sad reflection she saw if she mistakenly glimpsed herself in a mirror.

"Perhaps tonight they will let me die," she whispered. "God . . . if there is a God in heaven . . . let me die tonight."

a better life

Most of us do not live in the tormented world of a woman like Mary Magdalene. Before her encounter with Christ and her radical liberation from the spirits that tormented her, life was a living hell. There are women, however, and you may be one of them who live in a nightmare of a different kind. Whether it's an unfaithful husband, a world controlled by alcohol or drugs, the ravages of disease, or any of a number of issues that women have talked to me about, the torment you face day in and day out is real. I am amazed at the strength of women. Herbert Ross's movie *Steel Magnolias* was well titled, for it seems that so many women can stand under the pressure of a load that should bend them in two.

When you find yourself with a few quiet moments, do you ever wish that you were someone else? The desire doesn't have to be rational or something anyone else would understand. Maybe you yourself don't entirely understand. You simply long to be different. Better.

Of course, our ideas of better can differ. For some, it might mean physical beauty. For others, power or wealth. Or a combination. For some, it is simply to feel as if they belong in this world and that their lives have purpose and meaning.

Every culture carves out an ideal to worship just as surely as the children of Israel worshipped the golden calf in the wilderness. When it comes to the physical, those of us in the West usually picture a tall, ridiculously thin woman with teeth so white you could use them to land an aircraft in fog. For power, perhaps a corporate CEO smiling out of the pages of a magazine surrounded by cars and a mansion or one of those giant cherry desks that screams wealth. Whatever the picture of perfection, if we fall short—as most of us do—we are reminded daily through the media that we are not all we could be.

Most of us get to an age where we recognize God values our hearts far more than our dress size or wallet. But there are other more subtle comparisons that pull us down. Perhaps you look at someone else's marriage and they seem much happier than you and your husband are. You look at their children and observe how they behave in church while your children have the self-control of a herd of buffalo. You compare your relationship with God to a friend's and it seems as if God hears her prayers and treats her like a favored child while you feel like the tolerated stepchild.

Yes, I imagine at some point we all have reviewed the portfolios of our lives and wished for something different. Sometimes we realize we're being unrealistic or that we are falling prey to the siren call of our culture, and we let the dreams go. Sometimes we realize we're fine just the way we are. Sometimes we decide we can do something about our desires, and we make them happen.

But what if you can't do anything about it? What if you long to be something different, to have something different, and yet you know it will never happen? If you wake up every morning knowing that you need help to get out of bed and into a wheelchair, the choices you have are reined in. If you open your eyes to what your husband tells you is a beautiful sunny morning but the world to you remains as dark as midnight, then blindness has dictated what your possibilities are. I have several friends for whom some sort of physical limitation is the reality they deal with every day. Many have told me that in the midst of disappointment, they have found mercy—but they have had to mine at a great depth to discover these jewels of the darkness.

a severe mercy

Through my years of traveling I have met thousands and thousands of women. In each of the main cities on our calendar, there are a few faces I have gotten to know more than others. I see them every trip. We have a quick catch-up in my book line, a hug, and an exchange of photographs of our children or a quick prayer.

There are four people I have become especially close to. We write to each other at least once a week. These four are a mother and daughter, and a mother and son. Rosanna and Sarah, and Karen and Eric. Sarah's disability has her using a wheelchair, and Eric has Down syndrome. I have learned a lot from both families.

I am touched by Karen's honesty and Eric's kindness. My office at home is full of little gifts Eric has made for me. He is a very wonderful young man, but his health is a constant challenge, and he's often sick. Many times Karen has sent me quick e-mail prayer requests as she takes him to the emergency room. But despite his challenges, Eric has a very real tangible relationship with God and a deep awareness of heaven, and I cherish that in him.

From Sarah I am learning to step beyond what feels comfortable and trust God will meet me there. She has the gift of encouragement, and I will often open my e-mail to see a note from her letting me know she is praying for me. She has become very involved in her parish's prayer ministry and weekend retreats, and she has seen God use her life in many ways. Sarah has had to find the courage to move beyond physical and psychological barriers to live the life she knows she has been called to. She didn't ask to be born with spina bifida, but she refuses to let the limitations of her body define her. Sarah believes she is Sarah for a reason.

In fact, all four of my friends feel the same. None of them wastes time wishing he or she were someone else. Instead, their lives are filled with God-given purpose that overcomes any questions they may have about why things are they way they are. They know life is not random. Knowing that does not minimize the struggles they each face, but they face them honestly. I think that is probably one of Karen's greatest gifts to my life. She is not afraid to ask hard questions or pour out her emotions when they are at their most raw. As a mom she hurts when Eric hurts, but she celebrates the gift that Eric is to her life and to the lives of everyone who knows him. I believe that Karen is able to celebrate at a great depth because she is also able to pour out the bitterness and disappointment that could so easily consume her.

If you look at difficult physical challenges in your own life or the life of a friend or loved one, are they mistakes? The psalmist certainly didn't think so. Listen to his song of praise to God:

> Oh yes, you shaped me first inside, then out;
>   you formed me in my mother's womb.
> I thank you, High God—you're breathtaking!
> Body and soul, I am marvelously made!
> I worship in adoration—what a creation!
> You know me inside and out,
>   you know every bone in my body;
> You know exactly how I was made, bit by bit,
>   how I was sculpted from nothing into something.
> Like an open book, you watched me grow from conception to birth;
>   all the stages of my life were spread out before you,
> The days of my life all prepared
>   before I'd even lived one day. (Psalm 139:13–16 MSG)

Before you were able to take your first gasp of air, God knew every bone in your body. That means he knew the ones that were forming correctly and those that were not. He knew I would have brown eyes and Barry's would be blue. He knew the eyes that would be green but never see and the limbs that would not work and the ears that would not hear. He knew us all, and he gloried in us. How then could we presume to believe we should be different, no matter the difficulties in our roads?

a random place?

What if our longing is not for relief from the physical body but simply to be anything other than what we are, where we are?

No one gets to choose where she is born or who her parents are. One child is born into great wealth and favor, and another child opens his eyes into a world of poverty and AIDS in a small village in Africa. One child is welcomed into loving arms, while another is unwanted and unloved.

In your own life, perhaps you longed to be the girl at the table next to you. Or the woman down the street or across the country. The one who appears to have everything she could ever want or need—and more. But instead you feel trapped in a life not of your choosing.

Again, is any of it an accident? I know for sure that in God's original plan, life was never meant to be this way. The brokenness we suffer was not God's choice but ours. When Eve, made in the image of God, reached outside the life he had lavished on her, we all fell. Now the whole planet limps and weeps along.

But in the midst of all of that, I believe you are you for a reason. You are not an accident; you are a woman with an eternal destiny. It takes some of us a long time to understand that. Often it means letting go of what we think should have been and bowing our hearts to the sovereignty of God. He can take the least likely of lives and love large through them. Just ask Mary Magdalene, the tormented one.

We don't know very much about Mary Magdalene's past. All we know is that when she met Jesus, she was possessed by seven demons. Some people have confused her with the woman who washed Jesus' feet at Simon the Pharisee's home and have therefore assumed she was a prostitute. Mary was not a prostitute; she was a tormented woman.

I cannot imagine what it must have been like for her to be afflicted in such a way. Any who saw her would have assumed her to be mad or dangerous, and they'd have kept their distance. But even if she was ostracized by the physical world, there would have been no rest for her soul. Who knows what the demons did to her in the long hours of the night? I have never met a demon-possessed person (that I am aware of), but it must be a horror. To be taken over by the prince of darkness and his twisted cohorts would be a relentless agony of soul and spirit. Satan and his emissaries hate all that God loves and take delight in tormenting them. It must have seemed to Mary that there was no way out of the nightmare that was her life.

Thankfully, Jesus rescued Mary from the kingdom of darkness and put her feet on a path right beside his. And because of who she was and what happened to her, she was given a front-row seat in our Messiah's life. She was able to travel with him and see and be a part of his ministry.

> He continued according to plan, traveled to town after town, village after village, preaching God's kingdom, spreading the Message. The Twelve were with him. There were also some women in their

> company who had been healed of various evil afflictions and illnesses [including] Mary, the one called Magdalene, from whom seven demons had gone out. (Luke 8:1–3 MSG)

Mary Magdalene remained with Jesus until the bitter end. She saw all the moments of wonder, when miracles were performed and lives transformed. She also saw when Jesus was handed over to the soldiers and then to his own people. And she was there when he died.

When Joseph of Arimathea offered his tomb for Christ's burial, Mary followed. She watched as Joseph wrapped Jesus' body in clean linens, laid him inside, and rolled a stone in front of the entrance. Joseph went home, but Mary stayed for a while. Her heart must have been broken to see the One she loved so much beaten and mocked and crucified.

Of all those who followed Christ, Mary knew in a way that no one else did what was at stake. This beloved One who now lay on a cold slab was the same Jesus who had banished seven demons from her life. As she sat there that night, did she wonder if they would come back now? Would she once more be the punching bag for the kingdom of darkness? Was she alone again?

you are not an accident

Mary's story is one of the most eloquent examples of the truth that when Jesus redeems your life, it is changed forever. That doesn't necessarily mean that all your external circumstances change, but because the risen Christ is present, life is full of purpose and hope. Perhaps that is one of the greatest lessons I am learning. I used to think that when you love and follow Christ, he would change your life circumstances that are painful or clear your path of potential potholes. I believe now that the truth is far greater. Rather than get us out of trouble, Jesus lives in us through any troubles.

Mary was the first to see the risen Messiah. I am in awe of the grace of this gift. Jesus chose Mary to be the first to see that he had risen from the dead. He showed the one who had been tormented by the legions of hell that Satan, her enemy, was defeated and that he, Jesus her Lord, held the keys to life and death.

Before dawn broke that morning Mary made her way back to the garden tomb with anointing spices for the broken body of Jesus. As she got closer to the tomb, she knew that something was wrong. When she left there on Friday night, the entrance to the grave was sealed with an enormous stone, but now the stone was moved out of the way. She had no idea who would have done such a thing; why would anyone want to steal Jesus' lifeless body? Panic seized her and she turned and ran as fast as she could until she found Peter and John and told them that Jesus' body had been taken.

Mary followed them back to the garden. When she got there, Peter was inside the tomb and John stood at the entrance. It was true. The body was gone, but the cloths they had wrapped his body in were still there. Peter and John went home to tell the other disciples that the body had been taken and to come up with some sort of a plan to find out what had happened. But Mary stayed on her knees, weeping at the entrance to the last place where she had seen Jesus.

Suddenly, Mary heard a man's voice ask her a question. She turned to see who it was. The man was asking her why she was crying and what she was looking for. Mary wondered if he had something to do with the disappearance of Jesus' body. She begged him to tell her. "I just want to take care of his body," she pleaded. Jesus had given her a life again, and the thought that his battered body might be lying somewhere, uncared for, was more than she could bear. And then he spoke her name! There was no doubting that it was Jesus (John 20:15–17).

Can you even begin to imagine what that moment was like for Mary? She had watched the man who saved her life being beaten and executed. She had been there as his battered and broken body was put to rest. This was all she had left; the bitter blessing of anointing his body with myrrh and aloe—but even that had been taken away from her. In agony of soul, she reached out to a stranger for help . . . and found herself at the wounded feet of Christ, who spoke her name. There is something so deeply personal and intimate about hearing someone say your name. Only a few moments before Peter had been there, John had been there, but Jesus chose to show himself first to Mary. She was chosen to be the first evangelist!

I don't know how you view your life or the events that have brought you to where you are today. I don't know how inadequate you may feel or what physical ailments you may have. But I do know that there is nothing about your life that is an accident. When we look only at external circumstances, we are in danger of missing the whole point of the miracle and gift of the life we have been given.

After the death and resurrection of Christ, Pilate was still in power, Herod still ruled, and the Roman soldiers still rode their horses through the streets of Jerusalem—but everything had changed. When you know that the God who holds the universe in place knows all that is true about you and loves you enough to die for you, how could life ever be meaningless again?

deliverance discovered

1. In what ways do you tend to judge your worth by your circumstances?
2. Do you believe God made you just as you are with no mistakes? If so, why? If not, why not?
3. What do you believe about how Jesus values your life?
4. Is there something about your life that you think is an accident? If so, ask God to help you see it as he sees it.

a prayer of deliverance

Father God,

I am overwhelmed by the great love that you show to those of us who feel we do not measure up. Thank you that Jesus showed everyone that he loves and values the gift we are to His body. I ask you now in the powerful name of Jesus to help me see my life as you see it. Deliver me from the lies of the enemy. Help me to love my life as you love it. I am ready to let go of everything I have been told and embrace the truth.

In Jesus' name, amen.

TWELVE

i was made for this

Don't be ferocious with yourself because that is treating badly a precious (if imperfect) thing which God has made.

—Evelyn Underhill

Not only do we know God through Jesus Christ, we only know ourselves through Jesus Christ.

—Blaise Pascal

What is man that You are mindful of him,
Or the son of man that You take care of him?
You have made him a little lower than the angels;
You have crowned him with glory and honor,
And set him over the works of Your hands.
You have put all things in subjection under his feet.

—Hebrews 2:6–8

I'm no longer calling you servants because servants don't understand what their master is thinking and planning. No, I've named you friends because I've let you in on everything I've heard from the Father. You didn't choose me, remember; I chose you, and put you in the world to bear fruit, fruit that won't spoil.

—John 15:15–16 MSG

She looked at the dress lying on the bed, and it was all wrong. The style was wrong and the color did nothing for her fair skin. She tried it on, and although it fit, it seemed to hang on her as if mocking her shape. She wished she didn't have to go, but she knew how that would hurt her mother's feelings. Her mother had been so excited to show her the dress. Working on such a small budget, it was a miracle her mom been able to buy anything at all. She would have to go.

She knew how it would be, for she had lived these kinds of moments before. She would stand at the edge of the crowd and try not to make eye contact with anyone. She might offer to help with the refreshments so that she looked busy, and she would get through it as she had done before.

The dance hall was beautiful, lit up like a Christmas tree. Music called to everyone to find a partner and take to the floor. She kept her eyes on her shoes, which didn't match her dress. She was aware of the sounds of laughter and excitement all around her.

But then everything suddenly hushed. She looked up to see what had happened and there he was. Standing in front of her was a beautiful young man holding out his hand to her.

"I . . . I can't dance," she said.

"Oh, yes you can," he replied. "You've always been able to dance. You just didn't know it."

chosen

I will never forget the night I was baptized in my home church in Ayr, Scotland. I was sixteen years old, and there were several of us being baptized. Before the service began, we changed into our long white robes and met with our pastor, Reverend Edwin Gunn. He told us how things would progress in the service and what a special night this was in all of our lives.

We filed into the church and sat in the front row, which had been reserved for us. As the first hymn began to play, I started to weep. I couldn't stop. I was overwhelmed with an awareness that I was doing something Jesus had asked me to do and in that very act of obedience his presence and his delight seemed so tangible.

When it was time for the baptisms, we made our way to the stairs at the side of the baptismal tank. One by one, each person climbed the stairs and went down into the water. When it was my turn, I was shaking so much I could hardly get down the other side. I stood in the water as Pastor Gunn took my hand. Before he baptized me, he said, "Sheila, I asked the Lord for a verse for you and he gave me this: 'You did not choose me but I chose you. And I appointed you to go and bear fruit, fruit that will last, so that the Father will give you whatever you ask him in my name'" (John 15:16 NRSV).

With that, he lowered me into the water.

When I came up it was all I could do not to shout and dance (which is hard to do with a soaking wet robe clinging to you). I felt as if I had been kissed by God.

God chose me. I couldn't get that wonderful truth out of my heart. No one had ever chosen me before. I wasn't good at sports, so if anyone was asked by our gym teacher to pick a team, I was always at the bottom. When the boys had to pick a partner to practice for the school dance when I was sixteen years old, I had to wait for quite some time as the last few reluctant and awkward boys took what was left.

Chosen by God . . . now I just had to work out what that meant. Did it mean that from this point on in my life everything would fit neatly into place? Did it mean all my imperfections would be perfected? I'm a little embarrassed by this admission now, but I even wondered if perhaps, as I came out of the water that night, I would be changed. I thought it possible that my skin might have cleared up and I might have left a few unwanted pounds in the water.

I wanted an outward expression of an inner truth. Surely if God chose me, then he might want to make life a little easier for me. I guess I thought that being a "new creation" would show up on the surface (2 Corinthians 5:17). If I was leaving my old self in the water symbolically and being raised to a new life, then maybe I would look "new" on the outside.

I have come to understand that what Jesus wanted was to live his life in and through me, not to fulfill a few teenage dreams that might have changed my outer appearance but done nothing for my heart. Jesus was inviting me to join him in a dance that would take me through all the seasons of life.

Perhaps no one had an opportunity to understand that more than Jesus' own teenage mother. In many ways, Mary was still a child herself. When the angel announced that she would bear the Son of God, she was likely only thirteen or fourteen. And, as parents usually arranged marriages back then, she had probably been betrothed to Joseph since she was a little girl.

Betrothals were not like engagements. Betrothals were legally binding contracts. Although the couple didn't live together until after the wedding, it would require a divorce to nullify the contract. If Joseph had died before the wedding, Mary would have been considered a widow even though she would still have been a virgin.

Into this neat, small world the angel Gabriel—known as "one who stands in the presence of God"—brought a revolutionary announcement: "Rejoice, highly favored one, the Lord is with you; blessed are you among women!" (Luke 1:28).

Mary had no preparation for this enormous life change. One

day she was simply a good Jewish girl who did her best to be obedient to her parents, and the next moment she was visited by Gabriel. This supreme angel appeared only four times in Scripture. Each time it was to bring a message directly from the throne of God to a specific human being. Twice he appeared to Daniel (Daniel 8:15–27; 9:20–27), once to Zacharias to announce the birth of John the Baptist (Luke 1:8–20), and once to this sweet teenager, Mary (Luke 1:26–38). Mary is the only female in human history to receive a message from Gabriel.

The reason I chose this amazing young woman to help us realize what embracing our God-given destiny looks like is that her life combined the joy of the call and the heartache of the call. But first, the joy!

> Good morning!
> You're beautiful with God's beauty,
> Beautiful inside and out!
> God be with you. (Luke 1:28 MSG)

Can you imagine such a greeting! One minute she is sweeping the floor, wondering if she will see Joseph later that day, and the next thing she experiences is blinding light filling the kitchen and a creation not of human flesh filling the room. I have no idea what Gabriel looks like, but I'd guess he's pretty impressive. And here he was telling this young girl that in God's eyes she was beautiful inside and out. That speaks volumes about Mary. Not only was she a lovely girl to look at, but she was beautiful inside too.

As you can imagine, such an unexpected and magnificent visitor stunned Mary: "She was thoroughly shaken, wondering what was behind a greeting like that" (Luke 1:29 MSG).

I'm sure to say she was stunned would be an understatement. God had been quiet for a long time since the close of the Old

Testament. Mary learned from her mother and father (girls at that time didn't learn at the temple but rather at the knees of their parents) what God had said through the prophets, but for four hundred years since the completion of the book of Malachi, God had been silent.

Think about it this way: if you read through the end of the Old Testament and then begin the New Testament, it's almost as if you fell asleep during a movie and when you woke up you didn't recognize the characters now on screen. You sat there wondering what happened to the ones who were there before you nodded off.

Just before your eyes closed, God's people, called the Jews, had been kicked around by a lot of people. But many of them were now back in their land, although under the thumb of Persia—their land had been seriously reduced to Jerusalem and the surrounding areas. They had a temple, but it was nothing compared to the one built by Solomon.

When you opened your eyes, you found you'd fast-forwarded four hundred years. The region was now known as Judea, and the Persian landlords had been replaced by the Romans. There was no Jewish governor, but a high priest; and Jewish law was watched over by the Sanhedrin. There had not been a prophet since Malachi, but now they had the synagogue as a place for prayer and where men and boys could study the Torah.

It was in this world that Gabriel greeted Mary. Her response was a beautiful testimony to the preparation God does in the life of his children before he reveals his call:

> My soul magnifies the Lord,
> And my spirit has rejoiced in God my Savior.
> For He has regarded the lowly state of His maidservant;
> For behold, henceforth all generations will call me blessed.
> For He who is mighty has done great things for me,

And holy is His name.
And His mercy is on those who fear Him
From generation to generation.
He has shown strength with His arm;
He has scattered the proud in the imagination of their hearts.
He has put down the mighty from their thrones,
And exalted the lowly.
He has filled the hungry with good things,
And the rich He has sent away empty.
He has helped His servant Israel,
In remembrance of His mercy,
As He spoke to our fathers,
To Abraham and to his seed forever. (Luke 1:46–55)

This song of praise seems to have been modeled on Hannah's prayer in 1 Samuel (2:1–10). It also quotes from twelve Old Testament passages. Mary was obviously a devout young Jewess. And it's clear that although the circumstances were not what she might have imagined, she was ready to do whatever her God wanted her to do. With his help and strength, she was ready, willing, and able.

The same could probably not be said about her family—at least at first. Although there is a lot that is left unsaid about Mary's next few months, I think there are several things we can assume . . .

How must this have seemed to her parents? And Joseph's? Even the most trusting of parents with the best child in the neighborhood would be stretched to believe that an angel—and not just any angel, but Gabriel himself—had chosen to speak to a thirteen-year-old girl. Not only that, he had given her news that would put the families in a place of public shame and disgrace. How could that possibly have come from God?

Knowing Mary was a good girl with a pure heart, it must have been devastating for her to face questioning and surreptitious looks from skeptical neighbors. What must have balanced that out was the knowledge that she had been chosen by God to carry his Son. We are told she "kept all these things and pondered them in her heart" (Luke 2:19). She must have pondered a lot in those days, trying to understand God's plan.

a sword thrust through the heart

Mary carried her precious baby to term and bore him in humble surroundings. She must have been so proud, so captivated by her son. It can only be imagined how often she looked at his tiny face, counted his toes and fingers, and wondered what his future would bring. She would soon have an inkling.

When a Jewish baby boy was born, he was circumcised when he was eight days old. The mother was considered unclean for an additional thirty-three days. (Sixty-six if it was a girl!) Mary and Joseph took baby Jesus to the temple to ceremonially offer him to God, as he was a firstborn son. A wealthy family would bring a lamb as an offering, but Mary and Joseph brought two doves, an acceptable gift for a poor family.

While they were there they met Simeon, part of the righteous remnant of God waiting for the Messiah to come. God had told Simeon he would not die until he saw God's promised one with his own eyes. He took the baby in his arms and blessed him, but then he turned to Mary and uttered words that must have hurt her heart: "This child marks both the failure and the recovery of many in Israel, a figure misunderstood and contradicted—the pain of a sword-thrust through you" (Luke 2:34 MSG).

What did Mary make of that statement? Simeon was basically telling her that her beloved little lamb would be misunderstood and opposed. The Greek words used in this phrase communicate that through the controversial life of her son, many would be brought to the place of total collapse while others would experience a virtual resurrection. It was clear that a clash of great magnitude was in his future. Even as she held her son in her arms, Simeon told her a sword would pierce her heart.

It must have made her ache to think of what the future held. Did she question why God would choose her to mother his Son, only to see him harmed? Did she struggle to remain true to her promise of faith? Did her deep sense of knowing that she had been chosen for this unique role in history sustain her in moments like these? Knowing that we were made for something doesn't always make it easy or even always feel right.

This uncertainty likely remained through the next twelve years. We know little about Mary's and Jesus' lives during that time. We can be sure that they went through the joys and heartaches any family faces. Mary had more children, so Jesus got to be a big brother. He helped his dad in his carpentry work, and life went on. I think they had twelve years of relative normalcy until the day Jesus went missing and the larger drama began to unfold.

It's every parent's nightmare to lose sight of their child for even a moment in a crowded place, but Mary lost sight of Jesus for three whole days. In those days it would be normal for young children to travel with their mother and older children with their father. Jesus was kind of caught in between. Twelve was a transitional year for a boy, and it would have been his choice to travel with Mary or with Joseph. We are not sure what happened other than Mary assumed he was with his dad and Joseph made the same presumption about Jesus being with his mother. When they eventually realized he wasn't with either, they headed back to Jerusalem and found him sitting with the teachers and scholars in the temple.

Not only was Jesus listening to what they had to say, but he was adding his own comments and questions, the depth of which astonished the teachers. When Mary saw him, she was very upset and told him so. His answer must have stung: "Why were you looking for me? Didn't you know that I had to be here, dealing with the things of my Father?" (Luke 2:49 MSG).

That question, "Why were you looking for me?" is the same language pattern used just twenty-two chapters later when we read, "Why do you look for the living among the dead?" This appears to be the first time that Jesus attempted to instruct his mother and father about his divine mission and purpose. He was saying, in essence, "Where else would I be but in my Father's house?" Mary and Joseph had looked all over Jerusalem for him, but he was telling them that they should have come directly to the temple, for that is where the Son of God would be found. It is striking to read that Jesus was not standing among the elders, doctors, and teachers but was seated with them as an equal. There seems to be a gentle rebuke in Jesus' words to his mother: "Didn't you know that I had to be here, dealing with the things of my Father?" This was Jesus' first messianic statement to his mother, and I believe it must have hurt her at a deep level. In that short phrase, there was so much unsaid.

- "I belong to you, but I don't belong to you."
- "I am your son, but I am not your son."
- "You have hopes and dreams for me, but there is a plan beyond yours."

There would be many such moments for Mary as Jesus began his ministry. One day a woman deeply moved by Jesus' teaching cried out the words every mother loves to hear, although perhaps not so descriptively: "Blessed is the womb that bore You, and the breasts which nursed You!" (Luke 11:27). Jesus' response was, "More than that, blessed are those who hear the word of God and keep it!" Even the normal, "Didn't you do well having such a son," moments were denied Mary.

The clouds were beginning to gather over her son's head and over her heart, but in those last days of Jesus' life, Mary was given an unusual gift. It is this gift that tells each of us who we really are and lifts our heads up high even in the worst of times.

What gift, you ask? How would Mary survive what was about to take place? What redemptive gift had God tucked into her life that would also change ours? Mary was about to discover that this beloved son would change her life for all eternity. She and Joseph had given him a loving home on this earth, but Christ was about to purchase for everyone who trusts him a home in heaven that no one could ever touch or destroy.

a chosen destiny

Destiny is hard to define by our culture's standards. We look at a boy who handles a football well and think, *He's a natural-born athlete.* We look at a girl whose beauty is striking and think, *Her looks will take her far.* Our destiny as believers is not so easily defined or short-lived. Mary knew that she had been chosen to be the mother of the Son of God. It would have been easy to assume that when Jesus was missing she should have looked for him in a palace, not in the temple. As she looked to his future, she might have seen him on a throne, not on a cross.

When I came up out of the baptismal waters, I looked for a change on my face; but God was working a change in my heart to see his hand in all the circumstances of life. That is God's gift to you at this moment. You are chosen and loved. Your future is safe and secure, bought with the precious blood of Christ. You may not feel like a princess most days, but that does not change the truth that you are.

deliverance discovered

1. Have you ever felt as if your life doesn't matter much? If so, how did that feeling affect your day-to-day life?
2. What does God's choosing of such a young girl to be the mother of his Son say to you?
3. Do you ever feel that although you know God has called you, the calling is confusing?
4. If you could sit down with Mary before the crucifixion, what would you want to ask her?

a prayer of deliverance

Father God,

Thank you for the life of Mary. Thank you that she modeled in her life what it is to be devoted to you. Thank you that she embraced what she must have known would be a painful journey. Give me the grace to see my life in an eternal light. Help me to embrace your call to me no matter how difficult the circumstances.

For Jesus' sake and in his name, amen.

THIRTEEN

sometimes my life feels like a cliffhanger

Fear. His modus operandi is to manipulate you with the mysterious, to taunt you with the unknown. Fear of death, fear of failure, fear of God, fear of tomorrow—his arsenal is vast. His goal? To create cowardly, joyless souls. He doesn't want you to make the journey to the mountain. He figures if he can rattle you enough, you will take your eyes off the peaks and settle for a dull existence in the flatlands.

—Max L. Lucado

The Lord is my light and my salvation;
Whom shall I fear?
The Lord is the strength of my life;
Of whom shall I be afraid?

—Psalm 27:1

Only he who can say, "The Lord is the strength of my life," can say, "Of whom shall I be afraid?"

—Alexander Maclaren

The remarkable thing about fearing God is that when you fear God, you fear nothing else, whereas if you do not fear God, you fear everything else.

—Oswald Chambers

He shall cover you with His feathers,
And under His wings you shall take refuge;
His truth shall be your shield and buckler.
You shall not be afraid of the terror by night,
Nor of the arrow that flies by day.

—Psalm 91:4–5

"You should be able to do this," he said. "I was told you had all been practicing for weeks."

A few of the other divers who were already in the water acknowledged that was true.

"So what's your problem?" he asked her as she stood at the very edge of the diving board.

She looked at the water and then she looked at his face.

"Come on, just jump," he said, attempting to be encouraging. "You can do this."

She looked at the others in the water, splashing around and laughing as if they had just bungee-jumped off Mount Everest.

"If you're not going to jump," he continued, "then clear the board for the other divers."

Slowly she made her way back to the stairs. But someone else was climbing up. She was trapped. She could not go back, but she was even more convinced it was impossible to go forward.

She sat in the middle of the diving board with her head buried between her knees, hoping that she might simply disappear.

why is it so hard to trust?

As believers, trust is foundational to our lives. And yet I think trust is very difficult. What does it mean to trust? Does it mean that we will never be afraid again or that fear would find its proper place; it would have a part in the play but not be the main character? I have been on a journey to understand the connection between fear and trust for a long time. I know that at times in my life I have been crippled by fear, but there has always been this strong call I hear inside my spirit: *Trust me.*

One of the first Scripture passages I ever committed to memory was, "Trust in the Lord with all your heart, and lean not on your own understanding; in all your ways acknowledge Him, and He shall direct your paths" (Proverbs 3:5–6). As a child, I would ask my mother, "Does that mean I do things that make no sense to me if I believe that God is leading me?" My mom did her best to answer that for an inquisitive twelve-year-old. Children ask very difficult questions! She tried to explain that when I honor God in the choices I make, he will keep me on a straight path. The trouble I had with that was my path didn't always seem straight, even though I was trying to honor God in my choices.

I have gone back to these two verses over and over through the years, and each time I do it's as if there is a little more light cast on to text. "All your heart" seems key to me now. If I trust God with "all my heart," then I leave no part of my heart open to fear. I think for a long time I trusted God with a substantial proportion of my heart but allowed fear to play a bit part. That seemed reasonable to me. After all, we live in a world of people who use us and abuse us; friends can betray us or husbands leave. God in his wisdom and mercy doesn't always stop the evil that makes its way to our door, so surely fear is part of life on this planet.

Yet evil has always walked this earth since the Fall. Jesus told us over and over again, "Do not be afraid."

To the man whose daughter died before Jesus could make it to his house he said, "Do not be afraid; only believe, and she will be made well" (Luke 8:50). To a gathering of his closest friends he said, "My friends, do not be afraid of those who kill the body, and after that have no more that they can do" (Luke 12:4). From Genesis to Revelation, there is a call from God the Father and Christ his Son—trust me; don't be afraid!

What do we say, though, to those who have had trust destroyed?

trust destroyed

The challenge to trust is exacerbated if we had our trust violated when we were at our most vulnerable. That's a hard bridge to rebuild, especially if we experienced any kind of abuse—mental, emotional, or physical—as a child. In such a situation, trust is the first thing that is destroyed, right alongside innocence. In our early years, when we're learning what "normal" looks and feels like, it is devastating to believe "normal" feels so bad and hurts so much.

It's not only children who can have their dreams of a love story marred. As I write, I have two friends whose daughters are going off to college. I know both girls, and I am excited for them. But even in that joy, I know they will soon have to face moments that have the potential to change their world. As they try their wings far away from home, they must learn to pay attention to the signals of who can be trusted and who should be avoided at all costs.

What about the woman who wrote to me to say that she has been doing her best to honor God all her life, trusting that at the right time he would bring her a husband? At forty-six, her fear is that she will always be alone and her trust in God has been worn away. Or the wife who has been trusting God for years for a child of her own and no child comes. You may have been waiting for years for a better job, but no matter how hard you try, the doors always slam in your face. I think of my mother-in-law, who trusted God for healing from her cancer but no earthly healing came. I think of a dear friend of mine who sent her daughter off to a Christian college, only to discover that she had been raped by a fellow student.

In such situations the inevitable question is, "Where were you, God?"

why is it so hard to trust God?

For those who have experienced such a situation, it's hard to wipe away the images that leave such smudge-prints on the soul. It can be very difficult to trust in people again. Heartbreakingly, many of those same people also find it hard to trust in God again. They withdraw from the only One who can truly make things right, somehow believing he's involved in their pain.

Understand me: I believe questioning God for the right reasons is healthy. God wants us to be proactive about our faith. But blindly pulling away from him serves no purpose but harm. God would rather we come to him and tell him we're having trouble with faith than not come to him at all. Let's go back to our text from Proverbs, this time in the words of *The Message*:

> Trust God from the bottom of your heart; don't try to figure out everything on your own. Listen for God's voice in everything you do, everywhere you go; he's the one who will keep you on track. (3:5–6 MSG)

This is God's promise to us—if we trust him and don't try to figure things out for ourselves, he will lead us toward faith. He knows we won't always understand the why of things. And he tells us that even if we can't trust others, we can trust him. (Although the harsh reality is that trusting God doesn't mean we will always be protected from the pain of life, just that our Father will be there with us in it.)

"But Sheila," you may be saying, "it's one thing to say it and another thing to be able to do it." I know! Once lost, trust is very hard to regain. We just don't want to be hurt. So how do we get from a stuck place to a place of being able to open up? The answer is realizing that learning to trust is a process. For some of us it might come easily, but to many of us it will take a long time to totally trust. Many of us have old messages etched into our hearts.

I did a little research on why people find it hard to trust and what some of the stumbling blocks to beginning that process of renewal are. These are some of the things women said to me:

- "I've been hurt too much in the past. God didn't keep it from happening, so I'm not risking myself again."
- "God still lets us get hurt by people we love."
- "People, even Christians, are just out for themselves. How can God allow that?"
- "When you trust God and open up your heart to someone and tell the truth, they just use it against you."
- "I trusted that God would bring me a mate, and he let me down."
- "I trusted God for a child. I have served him all my life, and he has held this one thing back from me but he lets teenagers get pregnant. How can I trust a God like that?"

As I listened to many women talk about why it's hard to trust God, a pattern emerged. It seemed to me that our ability to trust is tied to the wrong thing. If our trust is tied to God acting the way we want him to act, we will be disappointed. If we believe that God answering our prayers the way we want him to is the only way we can trust him, we will live miserable and confused lives.

But if we simply trust God, with no strings attached, wonderful things can happen. Again, I'm not saying we won't live through trials. Children learn to trust their parents, but it doesn't mean the experience will be pain-free. I remember when Christian was just a few weeks old having to hold down his legs as his pediatrician gave him an injection. I was horrified and convinced my son would never trust me again. But he did. The most powerful moment of that whole experience for me was that when it was all over, Christian reached for me to comfort him. He cried, and I cried. He cried because his leg hurt, but I cried that even though I had been part of that confusing and painful experience, he still looked to me for comfort. That surely is a picture of the trust our Father longs for us to know.

If you asked me when I was growing up if I trusted God, I wouldn't even have had to think twice. I would have told you emphatically that I trusted him from the bottom of my heart. But if that was true, why did I live in such fear for so many years? Why did I live my life as if I was waiting for the other shoe to drop?

the speed bumps of life

I am not what they refer to as a "chick flick" kind of gal. I don't usually like romantic comedies or movies where your dog and your grandma die at the end in each other's arms on the beach as the sun goes down. I like action movies or suspense thrillers. Now, don't get me wrong; I am not into the kind of tripe Hollywood serves up where there are more dead bodies at the end than empty popcorn boxes. I like intelligent thrillers that keep you engaged in trying to work out what is actually taking place. I like that in my entertainment. But I've not always appreciated that in my life. It's that trust thing again.

Take marriage, for instance. It can sometimes be a challenge. I don't think the reason is Barry so much as it is what is in me. By that I mean the tapestry of my own experiences. I wonder how different I might have been if my dad hadn't died when he was such a young man. My sister, brother, and I were all under seven at the time, so our memories of my dad are few.

More than that, I don't have any memories of what my mom and dad looked like together. Most of my memories from my childhood are of my mom doing her best to raise three children. She never dated, so I never saw my mom with a man in a romantic way. What I was aware of, though, was how much she loved and missed my dad. Instead of understanding that was a legitimate response because of how much my parents loved each other, I made a vow as a kid that I would never love anyone so much that if I lost them it would be devastating.

The vows we make as children are powerful and have far-reaching effects. This meant that for me, when Barry and I got married, I kept a little part of myself back. Anything he did that troubled me, I tucked into my "just as I thought" file. I wasn't consciously aware of doing that, because I had done it all my life. But unbeknownst to me, it greatly affected my life.

My other skewed thought was that if you ever decided to love someone with complete abandon, that's when they'd die. So I suppose you could see my first response as a kind of gift to my husband to keep him around a bit longer! If you follow my thought process to its logical (or illogical) conclusion, the moment that I ever totally loved and trusted Barry would be the moment he dropped dead.

Seriously, though, this twisted thought process treats God as if he were a cruel father and not the loving Father he is. Only a cruel person would destroy something we love just because he could.

These warped attitudes of mine ended up not just affecting my marriage, but my role as mother. When I became a mom, the stakes suddenly became so much higher. I could keep a little space between Barry and me, but I just couldn't do that with Christian. Every time he was hurt or sad or frustrated, I felt it right alongside him and wanted to make it better. Sometimes I would have nightmares about something terrible happening to him; I'd wake up in a cold sweat and have to go upstairs and check that he was okay. I was torn, because I'd taught myself for many years to hold back, yet I was completely unable to keep that promise when it came to my child.

God's grace invited me to change. And let me tell you, it was a blessing to let go of my fear and mistrust. Suddenly I was freed to simply love my husband and child, rather than expecting the worst to happen.

I'm not sure exactly when some of the changes I've experienced in the last few years began. I just know I am a very different woman as I write to you today than the woman I was then. Part of the change is that I have shifted my idea of what a "straight path" will look like. I used to think that when God said if I trust him, he would make my path straight, it meant without bumps or curves. Now I believe that it means my path is leading me home no matter how crooked it looks. The other major change is a deeper understanding of who I am being asked to trust. The longer I walk with my Father, the easier it is for me to trust him. I will not always like where he takes me but if it's where he's going then I'm going too. That's my prayer every morning now: "Father, today I place my hand in your hand. Wherever you are going, I'm coming with you. I won't always understand, but I trust your heart. I trust your love."

I think another part of the process began when I took a fresh look at Jesus' mother, Mary, in what had to be the worst moment of her life. Even for Mary, trust had its own learning curve. She discovered there was a calling on her life that was far greater than her calling as a mother. It was the calling to be a follower of her son, Jesus, the Christ. She had to let go of what she cherished more than her own life to embrace a higher calling.

at the cross

We have talked about the shame of a public execution. Those being crucified were usually killed just outside the walls of the city on a busy travel route so that everyone who passed could mock and add to the inhumane indignity of it all. As Mary stood watching them nail her boy to the cross, no one cried out, "Blessed are you!" Did Gabriel's words come back to her that day? *"Mary, you have nothing to fear. God has a surprise for you."* What a bittersweet surprise for it all to come to this.

If Gabriel's words were far away that day, I don't imagine Simeon's were. *"Yes, a sword will pierce through your own soul also."* What mother could bear to see her firstborn son executed in such a barbaric way, mocked and tortured? What had her trust in God gained her?

Even as Jesus hung on the cross in an agony of soul and spirit, he looked down and saw his mother. How often had he looked into those eyes as a child and known such love? How often had she loved him, cherished him, sung to him, and tenderly wiped blood from his knee when he fell running across the yard to tell her some news?

Now she could do nothing for him.

If Mary was fourteen or fifteen when Jesus was born, and he was now thirty-three years old, at the crucifixion Mary would have been almost fifty—my age. I can't imagine what she went through in those moments. She watched each blow as the nails went through his wrists. She listened as his executors tormented him. As the blood ran down Jesus' forehead, she must have longed to reach out to her boy and wipe it all away. Did she ask, "God, where are you?" Did fear overwhelm Mary's faith? She stood beside John, who had to literally hold her up.

And so Mary watched her son die.

an intermission

There is a startling intermission in Mary's story. One moment she was at the foot of the cross watching her son being brutally executed, and then the lights were turned off. We don't know what happened to Mary in the next few days. We know that John took her to his home, but what was happening in her life?

In some ways, it's odd she disappeared from the stage. She knew more about the divinity of Christ than anyone else on earth at that moment. Think about it:

- She had been visited by Gabriel.
- She had given birth to this son, having never had sex with a man.
- She precipitated his first miracle at the wedding in Cana.
- She had seen the miracles and the healings.
- She had "pondered these things in her heart" for thirty-three years.
- She had watched him be crucified.

When everyone else thought it was over . . . did Mary?

Perhaps like no one else, Mary trusted what she could not see because of what she could not deny. We don't know who told Mary the news that her son was raised from the dead. The next time we hear her name, she was gathered with the crowd in the Upper Room just before the Holy Spirit fell on them all: "They agreed they were in this for good, completely together in prayer, the women included. Also Jesus' mother, Mary, and his brothers" (Acts 1:14 MSG).

In letting go of her role as Jesus' mother, Mary was able to embrace her glorious new role as disciple, follower, and lover of Christ the Messiah and Savior. She relinquished a gift that she was given on this earth to receive a gift that would take her into her eternal destiny.

a happy ending?

You might be tempted to ask why this account of what happened to Mary was so liberating for me. I think it's because Jesus took what Mary believed about herself and showed her another path. She got the bigger picture. She had lost her husband and watched men torture and kill her firstborn son, so she knew pain and loss and the fear that her trust had been betrayed. But no one could touch who she was. When we see her last in the Scriptures, she was waiting with the other disciples for the promise of the Holy Spirit—she was going about her Father's business. She had known the joy of marriage and motherhood, but in the end her greatest call was to trust—as a disciple of Jesus Christ.

Dear reader, that means wherever you are in your life right now, the joy and purpose that Mary knew is within your grasp. You don't have to be afraid of what might happen to you, to your family, to your children, to your careers. You don't have to live in mistrust because of what happened to you in the past. If you can begin to grasp the magnitude of what Jesus offers, there will be peace *now,* in the midst of life.

I do not for one moment want to minimize the pain of what your life has brought you—or what might come. All I'm saying is there is a Rock we have been invited to build our lives on, and this Rock cannot be shaken. What Mary saw in the eyes of her son as he was dying was not fear or hatred—it was love. That is the greatest mystery and gift of all. We have not been put on some kind of spiritual endurance course to see if we can make it all the way home; rather, we have been placed on a path and asked to walk beside the love of our lives. If you are in a good marriage, I celebrate that with you even as I remind you that God's love is far greater. If you find yourself in a place of loss or disappointment, I long to remind you that you are loved more than you would ever have the wisdom to ask for.

This is the key for me: We are loved by the One who is love. We are loved by the One who has overcome the enemy. We are loved by the One who says, *Trust me.*

deliverance discovered

1. Which moments in your life would you identify as times when it is hardest for you to trust others? Which times are hardest for you to trust God?
2. How does fear play a part in your life?
3. Identify moments in your life when trust began to be eroded.
4. What would it look like for you to trust God with your whole heart?
5. What could be a first step for you in trusting God no matter how small it may seem?

a prayer of deliverance

Father,

Fear so often clouds my life. I am afraid of what tomorrow might bring and if I will be able to face it. I am afraid at times that my life doesn't matter. I compare myself to other women and often feel as if I don't measure up. Help me to see my calling as Jesus described it—I want to simply follow Jesus.

As I face my anxiety, I will bring it to you and leave it at the foot of the cross.

By your grace, amen.

FOURTEEN

God will prove it's a love story

All I have seen teaches me to trust the Creator for all I have not seen.

—Ralph Waldo Emerson

Hush! my dear, lie still and slumber,
Holy angels guard thy bed.
Heavenly blessings without number
Gently falling on thy head.

—Isaac Watts

Let us be like a bird for a moment perched
On a frail branch when he sings;
Though he feels it bend, yet he sings his song,
Knowing that he has wings.

—Victor Hugo

My help and glory are in God—
  granite-strength and safe-harbor-God—
So trust him absolutely, people;
  lay your lives on the line for him.
God is a safe place to be.

—Psalm 62:7–8 MSG

For God so loved the world that He gave His only begotten Son, that whoever believes in Him should not perish but have everlasting life. For God did not send His Son into the world to condemn the world, but that the world through Him might be saved.

—John 3:16–17

My sheep recognize my voice. I know them, and they follow me.

—John 10:27 MSG

She awoke very early in the morning, while others in the village were still sleeping. She knew that as soon as the sun was up, everyone would be in a frantic rush to see him. Today he was coming to their village.

She had heard all sorts of stories. Someone said that he touched a leper and the disease left him. Others laughed at the story, knowing that no sane man would touch a leper. She didn't laugh. She believed. For all of her life, she had waited for this one to come—and now he was here.

She tried to hurry, for it took her longer than most. She called her burden her "friend," but in reality it was nothing more than a dead leg that she pulled behind the rest of her body like a resistant child. The sun was up now, and already the heat in the air slowed her steps. A small group of village children ran past her chasing a ball, laughing and kicking up dust.

"I think that's the first thing I shall do," she said to her "friend." "I think I'll kick up dust!"

"Are you all right, Aurora?" a woman asked as she was about to pass her. "Where are you going?"

"I'm going to see him," she replied. "Down at the shore. They said he would be down at the edge of the shore."

"I'm so sorry, my dear," the woman said. "But I believe his plans have changed. The crowds were too much, so he has taken a boat to the other side. James has offered to take me over. I do wish we had more room. I'm so sorry."

Aurora sat at the edge of the road and tucked her lifeless leg underneath her dress. Her heart ached inside her chest.

"I believe you, Lord," she said. "If only I could have told you I believe you. Even if you had done nothing for me, I still believe in you."

She must have fallen asleep on her knapsack, for when she opened her eyes the sun was already beginning to set over the water. She sat up and reached under her dress to pull her lifeless leg into passionless submission. When she touched it she caught her breath, for there was movement and life.

Great pools of tears began to flow. She stood on her two feet for the first time in her adult life.

"I love you," she whispered. "Here is my offering."

Aurora danced and danced and sent clouds of dust swirling into the air.

a love story

I fell in love for the first time when I was nineteen years old. I was a student at the London School of Theology. My only experience with boys previous to this "fall" were hesitant crushes. I was a shy girl and had no confidence at all in my looks.

I remember the first time I saw him. I was sitting in the row behind him in chapel, so all I could really see was the back of his head and an occasional profile shot as he turned to say something to his friend. It was his laughter that caught my attention at first. I soon began to plan my attendance at chapel to ensure I just happened to sit behind him again. Most of the students were there to meet with God, but I had lower aspirations.

After a few months and the grace and mercy of God, we became an item. I had no idea that being in love could literally change the color of flowers or the sound of rain falling or make studying in the library appealing. I was convinced I had found the man of my dreams.

It took me more than a year to even acknowledge to myself that he was not perfect. In retrospect, I see myself as a desperate romantic who wanted to believe this person would make everything right that had been wrong. I wanted to believe he could take every wound that lurked in the dark lands of my soul and heal them.

I know now that I wanted him to do what only Jesus can do. I had placed him on an altar in my heart that must only accommodate our Father God. God is a jealous God, and when we try to put someone else in his place there will be a tumbling. For me it came on a bright, sunny fall morning.

I had borrowed a book from my boyfriend and wanted to return it before morning classes (and I'm sure I just wanted one look at his face to carry me through New Testament theology!). I knocked on his door, and he asked me to come in. We chatted for a few minutes, but as I turned to go he said, "Stop. Stand just like that with the sun on your face."

I stood still, assuming that he thought I looked lovely in the sunlight.

Then he said, "I must really love you, because when the sun is full on your face like that, your skin looks awful."

With that, he dismissed me.

The funny thing is I think he meant it as a compliment. But I was of course devastated. I knew I had bad skin, and I'd spent every penny I could afford on creams and lotions to make it better. I had talked myself into believing it wasn't as bad as I thought . . . until that moment when I realized when anyone looked at me, that's what he or she saw.

I never made it to class that day. I went back to my room and cried and cried. I was an ugly duckling and there would be no swan unveiling for me.

i still haven't found what i'm looking for

I tell you this story for one purpose: to illustrate what happens when we replace our trust in God with something else. I tried to let a simple, faulty young man take the place of a wonderful, pure God. I based my belief in myself on what this man said instead of what God told me about myself. And I was made miserable because of it.

What about you? Have you had any ugly-duckling moments? I hope not. I hope you have been loved and treasured since you were a child. Even if that is so, however, there's a lesson to be learned.

I have come to understand we were made with the ability to be totally loved by God and to totally love him. The problem comes when we forget the God half of that equation. If God is not present, there is a huge space to fill, and on this broken planet we tend to turn to what we can see to fill the void. Yet there's nothing big enough to fill a God-sized hole. Men are inclined to turn to work to fill the space, but it is never enough. Women tend to turn to relationships, but even the best are not enough. We were made for God's love, and nothing else will do.

Still, it's hard. When I first started touring America as a Christian music artist, I was part of the Sparrow family. The Sparrow record label was a labor of love started by Billy Ray Hearn in 1976. The early artists signed to the label were Jamie Owens, 2nd Chapter of Acts, Michael Talbot, Phil Keaggy, and many other amazingly gifted musicians. I felt honored to be part of what was a family more than an artist roster. One young singer who really touched my heart was Annie Herring of 2nd Chapter of Acts. I loved Annie's honesty. I remember a conversation I had with her one day backstage at an event. She talked about being lonely and that even though she knew Jesus loved her, she wanted someone with skin on.

I so understood that.

walking and talking

The reason Annie longed for someone "with skin on"—and the reason we all do—is because that's how it used to be when Adam and Eve walked and talked with God in the garden of Eden. There was nothing that came between them and God but love until that fateful day when they reached out for the forbidden fruit. Immediately, everything changed and they knew they needed to hide: "When they heard the sound of God strolling in the garden in the evening breeze, the Man and his Wife hid in the trees of the garden, hid from God" (Genesis 3:8 MSG).

Let's take a look at several aspects of that sentence as it relates to our trust in and relationship with God. One of the greatest gifts that was extended to Adam and Eve was to be able to walk and talk freely with their Creator. They knew no shame or guilt, and they never questioned themselves, each other, or their Father; therefore, "trust" was a given until they sinned. Once that rift in relationship occurred, they questioned everything, including themselves, and so they hid. The greatest challenge for Adam and Eve then and for us today is to learn to trust again based on God's nature, His love for us and not our fallen nature. We changed that day in the garden, but God never has and never will.

The Sound of God

Verses relating to "the sound of the Lord" or "the voice of God" are very common in the Old Testament. They are always linked to a call to obedience and the reward of the presence of the Lord. (for example, see Deuteronomy 8:20; 15:5; Psalm 98:6). God expected that if he spoke, his people would obey. If they did as he asked, they would be rewarded. If not, they would be punished. So God's people were inclined to listen for his voice.

What's sad is that in the beginning, there was no need to be concerned with obeying or not obeying, reward or punishment. In the beginning, there were only obedience and joy. Until the Fall.

After the Fall, when Adam and Eve heard the all-too-familiar sound of the Lord, they were unable to obey. Their response in the garden is a foreshadowing of what was to come. They hid from God's voice. His voice was always meant to be pure joy to his children, but sin changed all that. They no longer trusted.

The Wind

When reading the verse, "When they heard the sound of GOD strolling in the garden in the evening breeze" (Genesis 3:8 MSG), most theologians agree that the translation of "evening" is not accurate. This is something I only recently learned. Like many, I always assumed God was busy during the day and came to walk and talk with Adam and Eve in the cool of the evening—an enjoyable thought.

But an accurate interpretation of the Hebrew, according to Old Testament professor John Sailhamer, is "wind."[1] God strolled in the garden in the wind.

This gave me a totally different perspective on Adam and Eve's relationship with God in the garden. What it says is that God was as ever-present as the wind. Not simply at nightfall—or any other time of day—but always. Just as God spoke to Job out of the wind, so he spoke to Adam and Eve. Just as he spoke to Elijah on the mountaintop in a still, small voice he talked tenderly with Adam and Eve, his cherished children. More than simply checking in with them at the end of a day, God was simply there. Present. Always available to his beloved creation.

But now they were no longer available to him. Because they no longer trusted.

The Trees

In the beginning, the trees were a statement of God's amazing provision for Adam and Eve—within the trees was everything these two needed to survive and prosper. Yet the trees were also a sign of their rebellion. It was from a tree that Eve plucked the forbidden fruit. When they were put out of the garden, they were taken away from the Tree of Life. Trees mark our downfall and our deliverance.

But as Paul reminded us in his letter to the Galatians, it is on a tree that we were redeemed: "Christ has redeemed us from the curse of the law, having become a curse for us (for it is written, 'Cursed is everyone who hangs on a tree')" (3:13). Although Adam and Eve might not have known it, their journey through us, their descendants, leads from tree to tree, branch to branch. Adam and Eve hid from God, but Jesus placed himself on display on the cross so that we might always have access to God.

Adam and Eve lost their trust in the heart of God that day, but we have the opportunity to gain it back. When the weight of their sin showed them a picture of what they looked like without God, they feared that God's love was based on their perfect behavior. What we now know is that God's love for us is based on who he is. This truth can change our lives if we are able to receive it. God's love for you at this moment is not based on whether you remembered to pray for the people in China or led your neighbor to Christ. God's love for you is the very essence of who he is, and he cannot change.

the journey

Still, we long for a corporeal presence. What you and I are looking for is what we used to have in the garden when we were fully known and fully loved. To walk and talk with God—eagerly listening for his voice. Everything that we now have is a poor substitute. When Adam and Eve rebelled against the Father, they lost so much. They lost their innocence, their intimate relationship with him and with each other. All of us are part of that legacy.

We have to remember there is one constant—one thing that did not fall in the garden. *God's love for us did not fall.* God has not changed at all. Our ability to receive that love has been damaged, but not one ounce of God's love has diminished.

Unfortunately, that's the hard part these days—letting go of all the mistrust the world has granted us and simply falling forward into the arms of the Father who is always there.

So how do we get past our fears? One step at a time. One of my all-time favorite quotations is from the great devotional writer Oswald Chambers:

> Soak and soak and soak continually in the one great truth of which you have had a vision; take it to bed with you, sleep with it, rise up

> in the morning with it, continually bring your imagination into captivity to it, and slowly and surely as the months and years go by God will make you one of his specialists in that particular truth.[2]

What Chambers was saying is that everything you and I are looking for in this life is right there in our Father's arms—it's just a journey finding our way back there. And we have to be willing to take that journey.

Every day I have to choose to believe that Barry loves me and that I, in my frail humanity, am able to love him. More than that, I am finding comfort in the truth that in our good days and our bad, we are never alone. The love and grace of our Father are always with us. It is a journey toward letting go. By that, I mean letting go of all our expectations for ourselves and those around us and setting our fixed gaze on God our Father.

As Thomas Merton wrote, "Duty does not have to be dull. Love can make it beautiful and fill it with life."[3]

One of the greatest changes in me because of my walk with Christ is my decreased fear of what might happen. I don't mean that I think I will be spared from pain and heartache any more than you. But I know God himself will be with me, Jesus will walk beside me, and the Holy Spirit will bring comfort and strength. It is a glorious thing to be loved like that. I do not need to fear. There is no end to the love of God. As Frederick Lehman wrote in the glorious hymn:

Could we with ink the ocean fill,
And were the skies of parchment made,
Were every stalk on earth a quill,
And every man a scribe by trade;
To write the love of God above,
Would drain the ocean dry;

Nor could the scroll contain the whole,
Though stretched from sky to sky.[4]

So that is my prayer for you, dear friend. I pray that the love of God will compel you to let go of whatever you hold on to tightly and hold on only to him.

You don't have to take one more step alone. You don't have to face one more decision alone. You don't have to endure one more day of sickness alone. You don't have to cry one more tear alone.

You are loved, and you are never alone.

deliverance discovered

1. Can you identify any ugly-duckling moments in your life? How did they affect your perspective of yourself?
2. In what areas of your life have you found love disappointing?
3. When you think of God's love for you, how does that make itself real in your life?
4. In what areas of your life do you need to let go of a wrong understanding of the love of God?

a prayer of deliverance

Father God,

I stand in need of a fresh revelation of your love. I am tired of trying to find in others what can be found only in you. I believe that you love me, but I ask for a fresh baptism in your love. I ask that by the power of the Holy Spirit you would give me the grace not only to live in your presence every day, but to love your presence every day.

For Jesus' sake, amen.

FIFTEEN

we are what we believe we are?

Bear patiently your exile and the dryness of your mind. The time will come when I will make you forget these painful moments and you will enjoy inward quietness. I will open the Bible for you and you will be thrilled by your new understanding of my truth.

—Thomas à Kempis

Didst thou give me this inescapable loneliness so that it would be easier for me to give thee all?

—Dag Hammarskjöld

And the Lord God said, "It is not good that man should be alone; I will make him a helper comparable to him."

—Genesis 2:18

Oh, that I had perished and no eye had seen me!
I would have been as though I had not been.
I would have been carried from the womb to the grave.
Are not my days few?
Cease! Leave me alone, that I may take a little comfort,
before I go to the place from which I shall not return.

—Job 10:18–21

No one knew her little secret. She didn't want anyone to know. There was something about having the secret that seemed to give her power. The secret made the rest of her life possible. Without it she would be a screaming mess, but this outlet gave her a release from the meaninglessness and pain of her life.

Sometimes she would sit with the family and eat supper or go to church or visit relatives, none of which she wanted to do. But no one knew that. The secret kept her safe.

Sometimes she would sit in the mall and just watch people. Did they think their lives mattered? They went through the same routine day in and day out, and why? Were they pretending too? Did they have their own little secrets?

She suspected her father did. At church everyone respected him and praised his role as a strong, godly father. He accepted it all and tucked it into the pocket of his Sunday suit; but when that came off, part of him seemed to disappear too. There was a distance in his eyes that she recognized. She was sure he was as lost as she, but she could never talk to him about it. They didn't do that kind of thing in her family. No one really talked. They just made conversation.

Now the college situation was back on the front burner. Would she return this semester? Did she feel better after her little "spell"? Her mother told her she was just tired and that college girls stay up way too late. In her day it had been lights out at ten and no nonsense. She wondered if her mother had ever enjoyed nonsense in her life or if everything had always been so neat and proper.

The mental questions were beginning to make her heavy inside, so she slipped into the bathroom, rolled up the sleeve of her shirt, and made just a little cut. Not enough to do any real harm. Just enough to keep her sane.

self-hatred

Think for a moment about the people who really bug you. Not just someone who said something insensitive last Tuesday that ticked you off, but people who just bug you by their very existence. It might be a tone of voice or the fact that they always have to add their two cents no matter what the subject matter. It might be how they look or how loud they laugh. You may not even be quite sure why they bug you, but bug you they do.

It's an interesting exercise to try to figure out why. There aren't many people who bug me—I'm a pretty big fan of people. But when I asked the Holy Spirit to show me what was true for me, I came up with a couple of faces. When I thought about what it might be about them that rubs me the wrong way, the results were quite telling.

With one girl, it's because she is so *loud*! The kicker is I'm quite loud myself. It's an ongoing joke at Women of Faith that I laugh like a horse—a horse with a megaphone. I can't help it. If something strikes me as funny, I just roar. My son is now at the age to find that quite embarrassing, but what's a mom to do?

The other person who bugs me at times does so because she seems so needy. When I asked myself what exactly is it about that

that troubles me, I realized it's because she takes time from friends whom I want for myself. Now, that wouldn't make me needy, would it?

Why is it that the very things we struggle with in someone else are the very things we struggle with ourselves? The very intuitive Herman Hesse put it this way, "If you hate a person, you hate something in him that is part of yourself. What isn't part of ourselves doesn't disturb us."[1] You'd think we would be more compassionate with those people, but we seem to be less tolerant. It's as if we believe that if we can punish the behavior in someone else, then somehow there might be some kind of exorcism in our own souls. But of course it doesn't work that way.

I remember having very difficult conversations with a particular friend when he found out I took medication for depression. I had never seen that side of him before, and we had been friends for more than ten years. I found his animosity disturbing. He doubted my salvation, called me a stumbling block in the body of Christ, and said we were no longer friends. The outburst left me reeling.

Several years later, I heard through a mutual friend that he was being treated for depression. Suddenly I understood his anger. He was trying desperately to keep his own dark clouds at bay. And to him that meant denying the possibility of the same in me. As the great bard William Shakespeare wrote, he "doth protest too much, methinks."[2]

I have traveled across America from city to city, church to church, for more than twenty-five years, and one of the greatest issues I see is self-hatred. I know—that's a very strong term that might not sit well at first. Many prefer to call it low self-esteem. But, really, what those feelings are is a rejection of who we are; we believe that at least part of us is unacceptable. What else can it be called but self-hatred?

The fallout of self-hatred is isolation. If we know that there is nothing good in us, why would we subject others to our obvious lack? So we withdraw—we hold back who we really are because we know that if anyone else got even the vaguest scent of our true selves, we would be exposed and abandoned. It is more comforting to withdraw by choice than be asked to leave.

But where do we get those original messages? How does someone begin to despise and reject a part of who he or she is?

a lonely road

James Burtchaell in his book *Philemon's Problem* addressed this very question as it would impact the rearing of a child in a Christian home:

> From his parents a child learns of a God who strongly disapproves of disobedience and hitting one's brothers and sisters and telling lies. . . . When he reaches the age for high school, he finds that God's own interests have expanded: He is obsessed with sex and drinking and drugs.[3]

In other words, if we teach our children that those who are in authority over us are placed there by God, it would be natural for the child to assume that whatever the authority figure endorses is endorsed by God and vice versa. His observation is humorous but very thought provoking. Depending on the age and stage of your life, you receive different messages about what a "good" person looks like. Often for children, the list is a litany of things our parents tell us not to do. It is inevitable then to assume acceptance is based on behavior. If you don't do this, God is happy with you, but if you do cross the line, then God is mad. In actuality, only your mom or dad or teacher is mad, but God gets the bad rap.

Think about the way so much of what you believe God approves of is actually what your parents or your Sunday school teacher approved of. I grew up thinking God would be mad at me if I went outside to play on a Sunday, because that was our day of rest. So I would sit in a chair with a book thinking, *Well, I hope you're happy, God. I'm not having any fun at all.*

As I grew older, I began to question how much God really entered into the equation. I realized my frame of reference really boiled down to my mom's (and other authority figures') dictations. At that point, I reached a bit of an impasse. If it hadn't been God directing me all these years, how then was I supposed to know what he really wanted of me? I'd been listening to the adults around me rather than God himself. And now I had other influences. What about what my friends and peers thought was the right thing to do? If I'd blindly followed my mom, should I blindly follow them? Was I already doing so?

Suddenly I was adrift. What I believed about myself wasn't really as true as I thought it was. I began to doubt myself. Of course, if I'd just listened to God, who was there the whole time, all of this might have been averted. But I wasn't quite mature enough to make that connection.

For most of my teens, twenties, and thirties I struggled to feel as if I really belonged anywhere. On the outside I was successful, but inside I was unconvinced. Because I was directing my doubt toward myself, I began to dislike myself. And I didn't think other people liked me either. I thought they put up with me because they were Christians and it was required of them.

Now, some people may well not have liked me and that would have been theirs to deal with. But I put everyone on the same team, and I was on the other side. My assumption was that if people knew all of me I would face rejection, so I always held back. As a result, I was a very lonely person.

what do you see?

In my midthirties, God began to expose the lies I had believed and bring some light into dark places. His grace is an overwhelming gift. I began, bit by bit, to believe that God loves me, right now, as I am. Then Barry and I married and we had Christian and the healing went deeper and deeper. But still, every now and again, if I am tired or stressed, I can feel those old monsters begin to gather strength. I can walk into the greenroom backstage at Women of Faith and find that old song playing in my head.

> *You don't really belong.*
> *People don't really like you.*
> *People find you annoying.*
> *Just go off somewhere by yourself—do everyone a favor.*

In such moments, I have to choose to bring my will in line with God's truth and walk away from those thoughts.

When we allow our brokenness to make our choices, we withhold who we are and what we have to give to one another. One of Satan's tricks is to keep us so obsessed with what we used to believe or what used to be true that we don't live in God's grace right now. That kind of self-doubt is counterproductive. It keeps us wallowing in the past, alone and defeated.

God wants to set us free to love him and to love one another, to live in real relationships, bringing all of who we are to the party. But we can only do that if we believe—really believe—we are loved. When God looks at us, he sees a daughter he adores; but that's not always what we see, is it?

If you were to stand in front of a mirror right now and take a good, long look at yourself, what would you see? Not only that, but how would you feel about what you see? How self-critical are you?

If you've gained a few pounds, what do you tell yourself? How many times have you called yourself an idiot or a failure? How many times do you say things to yourself that you would never say to someone else?

Not only that, but how many times do you assume others are saying those things about you—or, at the least, thinking them? As I said before, for many years I struggled with believing others felt the worst of me, because I felt the worst of myself. Even now I must confess I am startled at times by the feelings that still rear their ugly heads in my life even at this age. Self-hatred is very isolating because we try to keep the part of ourselves that we despise away from public view, and we automatically assume everyone else must despise us too.

We were never meant to live like this. We were made to embrace ourselves as we are, just as God does. The problem is that we don't feel as though we can run to our Father's embrace either. Because not only do we project our negative beliefs onto others, but we project them onto God too.

what does God see?

If you are disappointed in yourself, you assume God is too. If your parents discovered when they visited you in college that you had a beer in your fridge and were verbally disappointed, didn't you think God felt that way too? If you missed a few Sundays at church and bumped into someone in a coffee shop who commented on your absence, didn't you also feel you had let God down? If your child's lowest grade at school was Bible class, didn't you wonder what you had done wrong as a parent and if God considered you a dunderhead? The negatives we receive from others we project onto God, and we walk through our lives thinking we have let him down and he is very disappointed.

The fact is we're wrong. Jesus told us flat out that's not how our

Father thinks. The Gospels are full of stories of Jesus taking the morality of the day and turning it on its head. Jesus never minimized sin, but he separated the sinner from the sin that had a hold on her. This means he might not like what you do, but he absolutely, unconditionally adores you yourself.

Think of the woman described in John's gospel:

> The religion scholars and Pharisees led in a woman who had been caught in an act of adultery. They stood her in plain sight of everyone and said, "Teacher, this woman was caught red-handed in the act of adultery. Moses, in the Law, gives orders to stone such persons. What do you say?" (8:3–5 MSG)

Now to set the story, Jesus had taught in the temple the day before, but he was back early in the morning teaching. This was a place for people to gather who wanted to hear from God, so here God in Jesus was.

Jesus had sat down. In those days only those who had authority to teach sat, so Jesus was sending a message: *I am who I say I am. I am here on my Father's behalf.*

Then the Pharisees came to Jesus, asking their question. More than trying to humiliate the woman, they were trying to trap Jesus. The Law of Moses declared she could be stoned. If Jesus said to let her go, he would show he had no respect for God's law, so how could he possibly be his Son? But if Jesus said to stone her, he would lose all the broken ones who followed him because he cared for the poor and the downtrodden.

Jesus wisely refused the two options offered him and instead turned the tables on those who sat in judgment on the woman: "The sinless one among you, go first: Throw the stone" (8:7 MSG).

This had to be humiliating for these religious scholars. Their legalism did not allow them to lie, so they could not act. They'd deliberately drawn a crowd, and yet here they were having to acquiesce. As they began to turn one by one and walk away, there must have been such a hush in the crowd. Can you imagine the common people who'd gotten up early that morning to hear Jesus speak? They'd seen an eyeful. First the drama of the sinful woman and then Jesus' apparent defiance of the Pharisees.

But there was a lesson as well. Jesus issued his invitation to the entire crowd—let him without sin toss the first stone. The individuals in the crowd looked around at one another. Surely one of them could pick up a stone. Was there not one righteous man in the crowd?

Yet no one stepped forward. Not anyone from the crowd, nor even one of the Pharisees who put themselves forward as an example of perfect faith. None was blameless.

Jesus showed every person there that when you despise someone for his or her sin, all you are really doing is shining a light on yourself. The woman had been caught in the act, so she had nothing she could say for herself. And yet neither did her accusers. They had to leave.

Jesus turned to the woman and asked where her accusers were. Keep in mind even speaking to her was a radical statement on his part, when most would have shunned her. There was no doubt about her guilt. Her sin was publicly exposed, but what Jesus had illustrated is that every one of us stands guilty before God. This must have been the first time in her life that someone leveled the playing field in front of her. I wonder what it did for her to have a man defend her? I imagine she was used to being used and looked down on. As far as she could see when the Pharisees dragged her by her hair through the streets, her fate was sealed and there was no going back. What Jesus did was give her a way forward.

When she told Jesus they had gone, he said, "Go on your way. From now on, don't sin" (John 8:11 MSG).

Do you see the grace here? Can you feel the gift Jesus gave this woman who had no human defense? He looked at the person behind the sin and told her she had worth.

Don't you wish we could really grasp hold of this in the church? Can you imagine what it would be like if we turned from being such a judgmental body to those holding out arms of love and grace in Jesus' name? We just have to believe it ourselves first.

the truth

The truth is that God is neither your mom and dad, nor your husband, nor the girl at work who is always critical of you. God doesn't look at you and think, *Did you mean to get your hair cut like that? Did someone tell you that you looked good in yellow? Couldn't you have done that better?* God adores you just as you are.

We are locked in for a time to a broken planet with a flawed system of understanding the purpose of our lives. I no longer believe, however, that we are stuck like this until Jesus takes us home. I believe he wants to set us free to live in his love right now. We just might have to do a little spring-cleaning first. So, I have a little project for you.

Take a piece of paper or a notebook and, with the Holy Spirit's help, write down all the negative things you can remember for as far back as they go. It might be from a Sunday school teacher or someone in your family. It might be from your parents or your husband. Wherever they came from, they need to be the things that made you feel bad about yourself.

I want you to take that list, and at the end of this chapter when we pray together, I want you to give it to Jesus and let his blood wash it away. Those messages don't belong to you. God adores you. He is not disappointed in you. You are his beloved daughter and he wants you to kick up your feet in the dust and dance.

deliverance discovered

1. What are the things you have believed from childhood about God that may not be true?
2. What are the small secrets you hide?
3. What does the story of the woman caught in adultery say to you?
4. Write down all the negative things you have been told since you were a child. Now tear up that list and ask God to help you see yourself as he does.

a prayer of deliverance

Father God,

I kneel before you now in the presence of your grace. I have believed so many things about you that are not true. I have projected things I feel about myself onto you. Please forgive me for accepting these things to be true.

Father, I bring these requests to you. They represent a wound in my heart and soul I want to let go of. First, in Jesus' name I choose to forgive those who wounded me. And two, I let go of wanting them to hurt as I have.

Now I give you these requests and I will not go back to them. In Jesus' name, I tear them up and throw them away.

Thank you for your love and grace. Thank you that you love me so much.

In Jesus' name, amen.

SIXTEEN

table for two, please

Accustom yourself to the wonderful thought that God loves you with a tenderness, a generosity, and an intimacy that surpasses all your dreams. Give yourself up with joy to a loving confidence in God and have courage to believe firmly that God's action toward you is a masterpiece of partiality and love. Rest tranquilly in this abiding conviction.

—Abbe Henri de Tourville

Do not keep the alabaster boxes of your love and tenderness sealed up until your friends are dead. Fill their lives with sweetness. Speak approving, cheering words while their ears can hear them and while their hearts can be thrilled by them.

—Henry Ward Beecher

No man is an island, entire of itself;
every man is a piece of the continent, a part of the main.

—John Donne

Love never gives up.
Love cares more for others than for self.
Love doesn't want what it doesn't have.
Love doesn't strut,
Doesn't have a swelled head,
Doesn't force itself on others,
Isn't always "me first,"
Doesn't fly off the handle,
Doesn't keep score of the sins of others,
Doesn't revel when others grovel,
Takes pleasure in the flowering of truth,
Puts up with anything,
Trusts God always,
Always looks for the best,
Never looks back,
But keeps going to the end.

—1 Corinthians 13:4–7 MSG

It had rained for weeks. Every time she peered out of the dirty window, the scene was the same. Rain bounced off the piles of trash in her yard. She thought about washing the windows, but what was the point? If she cleaned them today, they would be dirty again tomorrow.

"Why would I wash my windows?" she asked her cat, Snowball, as it curled up by the fire. "To get a better look at the rain? It would be a waste of time and effort. Just a waste."

She saw the note pushed under her door again and knew what it would say: "Let us lighten your load and brighten your day—no charge." She trashed the note as she did with every promise in her life that had proved to be too good to be true.

After supper she put the dishes in the sink and sat in her chair by the fire with her cat, Snowball, in her lap. On a small table by her chair was her mother's old Bible. It had been some time since she picked it up and read it, but she liked to have it right by her.

Suddenly, with unaccustomed energy, Snowball jumped off her lap and onto the table, knocking everything over in the process.

"Well, kitty!" she said. "That's the most energy you've expended in quite some time."

She picked up her magazines and the old Bible. It fell open where she had an embroidered bookmark in place. She read a passage that was underlined:

> Do not remember the former things,
> Nor consider the things of old.
> Behold, I will do a new thing,
> Now it shall spring forth;
> Shall you not know it?
> I will even make a road in the wilderness
> And rivers in the desert. (Isaiah 43:18–19)

She smiled. "We certainly have rivers in this desert!" she said to Snowball.

Turning off the lights, she headed off to bed. She felt something underfoot and realized that when Snowball made her grand leap of faith, she had knocked the trash over. There it was. The note promising a different life. She picked it up and smoothed it out. As she surveyed the dismal surroundings she had lived in for so long, she scribbled two words on the back of the paper: WHY NOT?

She slept for a long time. When she finally opened her eyes, it was only because Snowball was tapping rather insistently on her chest. She looked at the clock beside her bed and was surprised to see she had slept for two hours beyond her usual time. She got out of bed, stretching with one arm and scratching behind Snowball's ear with the other. When she stepped into her living room, she stopped. She couldn't believe what she was seeing.

Sunlight was streaming through spotless glass. She made her way over to the window and looked out at a glorious splash of color filling every flower bed.

I didn't believe it, but it was true, she thought with wonder in her eyes.

the overwhelming love of God

The New Testament is full of stories of those whose lives were radically transformed by the love of God. We have looked at the lives of Mary Magdalene and Mary the mother of Jesus—women who had a close and lasting relationship with him. For some people, like the woman caught in the act of adultery, we only know of one encounter. But the power of that one meeting was enough to change the direction of their lives. There were many such encounters described in the New Testament. Whether the meeting was brief or extended, the story is the same: Jesus takes us where we are and loves us back to life.

We see God's love poured out on a woman tormented by demons and a man who cuts himself with rocks in his agony of mind and soul. We see God's mercy transform a woman caught in the very act of her sin or another welcomed as she anoints his feet with the finest of perfume that represents her life-savings and dries them with her hair. On the cross, we see Christ's redemptive love reaching out to a thief who is in the very act of dying. The thief has no more life to live to show the fruit of his changed heart, but Jesus accepts him as he is.

I read the Bible with new eyes these days. In every parable, no matter who the main players seem to be, the story is about the love of God. It's not about us—about how good or bad we think we have been. It's all about our Father God and his beautiful Son, Jesus. I get that now.

Still, as clear as the message is, I'm sure if it were left up to us, some people would not get an invitation to dine with God. Take a man like Zacchaeus. If you are like me, you probably learned his story in Sunday school and sang the song:

> *Zacchaeus was a wee little man,*
> *And a wee little man was he.*
> *He climbed up in a sycamore tree,*
> *For the Lord he wanted to see.*

His story is a remarkable one because it shows there are no limits to the love of God.

> There was a man there, his name Zacchaeus, the head tax man and quite rich. He wanted desperately to see Jesus, but the crowd was in his way—he was a short man and couldn't see over the crowd. So he ran on ahead and climbed up in a sycamore tree so he could see Jesus when he came by.
>
> When Jesus got to the tree, he looked up and said, "Zacchaeus, hurry down. Today is my day to be a guest in your home."
>
> Zacchaeus scrambled out of the tree, hardly believing his good luck, delighted to take Jesus home with him. Everyone who saw the incident was indignant and grumped, "What business does he have getting cozy with this crook?"
>
> Zacchaeus just stood there, a little stunned. He stammered apologetically, "Master, I give away half my income to the poor—and if I'm caught cheating, I pay four times the damages."
>
> Jesus said, "Today is salvation day in this home! Here he is:

Zacchaeus, son of Abraham! For the Son of Man came to find and restore the lost." (Luke 19:1–10 MSG)

Many theologians consider Luke 19:10 to be the key verse of Luke's gospel: "For the Son of Man came to find and restore the lost." In that one verse, the entire mission of Christ is presented. Jesus didn't come to argue with the religious leaders or to heal those who were sick or to paint a more accurate picture of his Father. Jesus came to find and restore every lost human being. The phrase "the lost" can be translated here as "broken beyond repair." Jesus came to save those who believe they are broken beyond repair.

Have you ever felt that way? I know I have. There have been moments in my life when I've thought, *I'm not going to make it, Lord; I'm too broken, too despairing, too far gone.* I love this verse because it says to you and to me that if we feel that way we can take heart, because that's why Jesus came!

Is there someone in your family you have been praying for but you are beginning to despair over because he or she seems to get harder and harder every time you mention the name of Jesus? That's what Zacchaeus was like—a man with the hardest of hearts.

The great news about this story is that even though Zacchaeus went to get a peek at Jesus, Jesus came looking for him.

a hardened heart

Zacchaeus was not simply a tax collector; he was the *architelones,* the boss. He held a high office in the Roman tax system. He would have been above the apostle Matthew in rank. He made his money by extortion. If taxpayers owed the Roman government, say, $100, then Zacchaeus would demand $120 and pocket the extra twenty bucks. He was bleeding his own people dry.

He was based in Jericho, a major customs center, and the location was obviously working for him. Jericho was a beautiful place. Just to the southeast of Jerusalem, it was a rich and flourishing town, celebrated for its remarkable ring of palm trees around the border of the town.

That's where we find Zacchaeus. Because of his short stature, he climbed a tree to get a better view of Jesus, who was visiting Jericho on his last visit to Jerusalem. Passover was close at hand, so the road to Jerusalem was busy. Plus, the news that Jesus had healed a blind man had brought the curious out to see who this man was.

But why did Zacchaeus want to see Jesus? Why would a rich Jew want to see a poor itinerant preacher whose message was about self-denial? We don't really know, so perhaps we'll just put it down to curiosity. Jesus was the talk of the town, so Zacchaeus wanted to get a look. He had no idea that his whole world was about to get turned upside down.

There are moments in the stories of all our lives that are turning points. The decisions we make at those moments affect the direction of our paths. Just like a rudder on a ship can change its course, so too with those God-given turning points.

Zacchaeus was about to meet one of those moments face-to-face. We are given no indication that Zacchaeus attempted to get Jesus' attention. He was just watching the buzz below him when suddenly Jesus stopped, looked up, and spoke directly to him. It wasn't a casual greeting or a question. It was an imperative: "Zacchaeus, hurry down. Today is my day to be a guest in your home" (19:5 MSG).

As you can imagine, Zacchaeus was very excited to have Jesus as his guest. The rest of the crowd, however, was furious that Jesus would spend time with a man like this. They didn't get it. They didn't understand that, for Jesus, the fact that Zacchaeus was a despised tax collector was *the whole point.* Jesus had spent a lot of time talking about how difficult it is for rich people to enter the kingdom of heaven. But rather than hearing that it might be harder for those who have so much to let it go, the crowd instead heard simply that Jesus was for the poor and against the rich. It was a theme they would have held close to their hearts.

Imagine if your mother had been widowed for years and struggled simply to survive from day to day. Imagine now it was her turn to pay taxes. As she stood in front of Zacchaeus, he demanded more than she owed. The extra would cost her dearly. She would have to go without food for a few days. She might not be able to visit the doctor when she needed to.

But that's what Zacchaeus was like—a heartless, greedy man.

It's one thing to play Robin Hood and rob from the rich to give to the poor; it's quite another to turn the tables on those who suffer every day and make their lives worse. If I had been in the crowd that day, I'm sure I would have been very upset that of all the people Jesus could single out to eat with, he chose this parasite.

But that's not really God's concern. He doesn't care if his love is offensive to us. He simply says to whoever will come that they are welcome at his table. No one on this planet has to eat alone because Jesus has a table for two with each of our names on it.

Including Zacchaeus. Zacchaeus was stunned by the gift of the presence of Christ. But he was also aware of the unrest in the crowd. And he realized how much the people despised him. In a moment, life became crystal clear to him. What did it matter to have all that money but no peace? What advantage was found in being able to sit home alone and count his money but find it hard to sleep at night?

It was a lightbulb moment.

Zacchaeus showed the fruit of his change of heart. He offered to give half of everything he owned to the poor and return what he embezzled from individuals four times over. This amount was far above what Levitical law called for. In Leviticus, the people were told that if they had to make restitution it should be in the amount taken plus one-fifth of that amount added on (5:16). This meant, for instance, if Zacchaeus had stolen $100 from someone, by Jewish law he should give them back $120. But Zacchaeus said that to show where his heart was, he would give $400.

Then he welcomed Jesus into his home. And Jesus showed everyone how he considers every soul precious, every heart worthy of redeeming.

Jesus refuses to be boxed in. Just when we think we have a handle on how he works, he destroys that theory. Jesus came to seek and to save the lost. The lost are found in homeless shelters and in mansions in Beverly Hills. They are found on Wall Street and in Wal-Mart. They are found in my home and in your home.

I think in our fallen humanity we find some "lost" people easier to accept than others. Someone like Zacchaeus would probably not make our list. But he would make God's. There is no human being so lost that God will not invite him or her to a table for two. Zacchaeus wanted to see what Jesus was *doing,* but Jesus wanted Zacchaeus to know who he is. That kind of face-to-face confrontation across a meal table can change the hardest of hearts.

lost

Have you ever felt lost? It might be that you have wandered away from what you know is the right path and simply can't find your way home. Perhaps someone else dropped the ball and left you reeling. One woman I talked to recently, whose husband left her after thirty-two years of marriage, asked me, "What do I do now?" You may have deliberately walked away from God, and although you openly acknowledge that you feel lost inside, you're no longer sure that you will ever be welcomed home again. Jesus addressed each one of these situations with some incredible news!

The idea of being lost is a theme we find over and over in Luke's gospel. Luke 15 contains the parables of the lost sheep, the lost coin, and the lost, or prodigal, son. Each story builds on the one before, emphasizing the depth of the Father's love no matter whether we intended to walk away, were dropped and lost, or left in rebellion.

Let's take a quick look at each of these stories as it relates to God's love for us.

Wandering and Lost

In the story of the lost sheep (Luke 15:1–7), we are told that if a sheep wanders off and gets lost, the shepherd won't rest until he finds him and brings him home.

There are some of us who don't mean to get separated from the body of Christ. We just wander off for a while, seeing what's new in someone else's field; and before we know it, it's dark and we can't find our way home. Jesus tells us he will come looking for us, and he will not stop until he finds us.

I talk to so many women whose concern is for a child who has wandered away from the truth. They are not true "prodigals," since they live productive, helpful lives, but they have excised faith and relationship with Christ out of their lives. Jesus says, "I will go looking for this one when it starts to get dark and I will carry him home."

Dropped and Lost

What does the story of the lost coin tell us (Luke 15:8–10)? There are some whose lives are dropped and lost. Unlike the wandering sheep who have simply strayed from the path, these are people who have completely left the fields, headed in dark directions.

I have talked to many women who had a divorce dropped on them out of the blue, often after years of marriage. With no warning at all they went from a secure, normal life to being out in the cold, expected to find their way in the world and in the job market. One woman told me that it felt as if someone cut the string that held her life together, and she fell and rolled under the sofa—and no one even noticed she was gone.

The good news of this story is that you are never lost to God. Even if you have left your original life completely behind, he knows exactly where you are. When no one else sees or cares, he does and he will find you and help you begin a new life.

Lost by Choice

God's grace and love for us are overwhelming to me. Even when we choose to walk away from him, he is always waiting for us to come home.

The story of the lost son is not about the rebellion of the son but the heart of the Father. When the boy decides to return home, it's because he's run out of cash, not because he misses his father. He has his story all ready, but the father has his heart all ready. The father doesn't even ask the boy where he has been, what he did with the money, or why he is coming home now. He just welcomes his boy home and throws quite a bash in his honor. Even the party is not about the son being home; it is about the Father who waits and welcomes each one of us back into his arms.

fearfully and wonderfully made

I had been praying for a few days that the Lord would help me find an illustration to show how carefully we have been made and how passionately God loves each one of us. I feel it so deeply inside, but at times it's hard to translate that into words. Then I heard a message that seemed to fit the bill, showing one more layer God has poured his life and love into.

A friend suggested I should listen to a sermon on YouTube by Louie Giglio. The subject was "The Greatness of God."[1] So I signed in to YouTube and listened for a few minutes as Louie described an encounter he had with a molecular biologist. This scientist asked Louie if he was aware of the existence of a protein molecule in the human body called laminin. Laminin is a cell-adhesive protein molecule (I know—it sounds like Greek to me too) that literally holds us together. I decided to take a look for myself . . . and it's pretty breathtaking.

If you have access to a computer, it's worth looking this one up. If you Google "laminin," you will see that the shape of this tiny protein molecule that holds our bodies together is the shape of a cross. Isn't that amazing? This tiny little form is multiplied many thousands of times over inside our bodies. It can't help but remind us that God is ever-present in our lives—in the very marrow of our bones! The psalmist David wrote this before computers had even been imagined:

> Marvelous are Your works,
> And that my soul knows very well.
> My frame was not hidden from You,
> When I was made in secret,
> And skillfully wrought in the lowest parts of the earth.
> Your eyes saw my substance, being yet unformed.
> And in Your book they all were written,
> The days fashioned for me,
> When as yet there were none of them. (Psalm 139:14–16)

There is nothing random or "careless" about your life. God formed every tiny cell in your body. He determined if your eyes would be blue or brown, if your hair would be dark or blonde. Not one hair falls to the ground outside his radar. It is a great mystery to me that the cross is built into our DNA, and it is an overwhelming comfort. The Greek word *sozo* means "to save and to heal." Built into the very fabric of your being are salvation and healing. That is "fearful and wonderful" indeed!

I wonder how many other messages there are tucked into every aspect of our lives about the redemptive love of God. Lana Bateman, our prayer intercessor at Women of Faith, told me about an article she read in a medical journal by a molecular biologist who is also a brilliant pianist. He wrote that if you take the unique DNA strand that defines each human being and turn it on its side so that it resembles a piano keyboard, every human being has his or her own individual melody. Just think: God has written a song in your very soul.

My dear friend, I pray that God, by the power of the Holy Spirit, would reveal to you as no one else can just how *loved* you are. It is written into your very DNA.

deliverance discovered

1. Have you ever felt broken beyond repair?
2. Who is someone in your life who seems too far away for God to reach?
3. Have you ever found God's unconditional love offensive? In what ways?
4. What does the story of Zacchaeus say to you now that you may have missed before?
5. Reflect on the fact that the very cells of your body that hold you together are in the shape of a cross, and let the wonder fill you up!

a prayer of deliverance

Father God,

I am amazed that every part of my life is watched over and lovingly carried by you. Thank you that no matter whether I have had seasons of wandering or times when I have felt dropped and abandoned, you have always been there.

I bring before you now the names of those whose lives are heavy on my heart. Father, I trust you. They are on your timetable and not on mine, and you will lovingly go after them and bring them back to your side.

May your love be my strength today and every day.

In Jesus' name, amen.

SEVENTEEN

no light at the end of my tunnel

Lord, it is dark! Lord, are you there in my darkness? Where are you, Lord? Do you love me still? I haven't wearied you? Lord, answer me! Answer! It is so dark!

—Michel Quoist

"The dark night of the soul" is not something bad or destructive. On the contrary it is an experience to be welcomed as a sick person might welcome a surgery that promises health and well-being. The purpose of the darkness is not to punish or afflict us. It is to set us free.

—Richard Foster

The mass of men lead lives of quiet desperation.

—Henry David Thoreau

They despair of things ever getting better—they're on the list of people for whom things always turn out for the worst.

—Job 15:22 msg

Alongside Babylon's rivers
  we sat on the banks; we cried and cried,
  remembering the good old days in Zion.
Alongside the quaking aspens
  we stacked our unplayed harps;
That's where our captors demanded songs,
  sarcastic and mocking:
  "Sing us a happy Zion song!"
Oh, how could we ever sing God's song
  in this wasteland?

—Psalm 137:1–4 msg

For hours she had wandered in this maze of tunnels, trying to find the place where she entered with her group. They had been told to stay together at all times and that if anyone felt claustrophobic and needed to take a break, they were to tell the person in front and behind and be taken back to an exit by one of the official guides.

And yet . . . it seemed silly to disrupt everyone. For just a moment she'd felt a little light-headed and had pulled into a small break in the rock to sit until her head cleared. The dank smell of the cave and the oppressive heat had caused a wave of nausea to overtake her, and as she sat with her head between her knees, precious moments had passed. She meant to tell someone, but the moment she sat down she felt too weak to speak. And now that she felt some color come back into her cheeks and her breathing returned to normal, the group was out of sight.

She had been sure if she just kept moving, she would find them. But it had been hours now and she was still miserably lost.

Her backpack was heavy, so she unloaded everything that seemed superfluous, keeping only her flashlight, a few snacks, and her water supply. She put the rest of her stuff on the ledge at the side of the entrance to the next tunnel. "We can come back for it later," she said to herself, trying to keep her hope alive. "I'll tell the guide to just look for the pile of stuff with my lucky bear on top."

She wandered on and on until she was too exhausted to continue. Her flashlight was beginning to flicker, threatening to plunge her into darkness. So she sat for a moment and put her hand out to steady herself on the rock.

Only it wasn't rock. Without looking, she knew that she was touching her bear. She had wandered for hours and was back once more at the entrance to the same cave. It was at this moment that she lost hope.

when hope is gone

I began this book by telling you about something that happened one Sunday morning as I was getting ready for church. Now I'd like to tell you the rest of the story. As I looked at my reflection in the mirror that day, I felt overwhelmingly sad and discouraged. I had to pull myself together for Christian's sake, but I was miserable. When I heard God speak those words to my heart, they seemed impossible—*I will deliver you!* I couldn't see how. Barry and I were in real trouble. I had lost hope that we would ever be able to pull out of this dark pit. It was such a mess.

Let me give you a little background. A few years ago, Barry went through a time of deep depression. I know what that feels like, for I have been there. It is a dark and miserable battle. No one can predict how anyone will choose to fight this darkness or whether they will have the strength to even try to fight. Some turn to others for help, while others simply disappear. That's how it was with Barry.

He stayed in bed and kept the bedroom dark all day until it was time for Christian to come home from school. Then he would get up and make an attempt to be as normal as possible for Christian's sake. But after I put Christian to bed, Barry would vanish into a dark place for the rest of the night. I tried to encourage him to see a doctor, but he was very resistant. He saw no point, as he felt no hope. I just couldn't reach him. He was in a hole so dark and so deep, and it seemed to get deeper with every passing week.

When I went through my own depression years ago, the one constant was an awareness of the love of God. Barry did not seem to have that comfort. Because of his illness, he believed that God was through with him—that no matter how hard he prayed, God was not listening. He began to question the value of his life and if he would ever feel hope again.

I found this very alarming and talked with a friend of mine who is a doctor. He told me that if Barry said anything like that again, he needed to see a doctor right away.

I kept asking Barry if there was something he needed to tell me. The rift between us was so great that I felt there had to be something else going on. I have always believed that if we can tell each other the truth, we can by God's grace survive most things. But he wouldn't talk to me. I believe now that God in his mercy decided to let the truth come out whether Barry wanted it to or not. I just didn't see it coming.

the house comes tumbling down

Barry and I differ in our tastes in homes. I like small and cozy, while Barry likes elegant and Italian. But since much of our lives is based around my schedule with Women of Faith, my travels, and my writing, when it comes to things on the home front, I felt Barry should have the greater say. I am honestly happy living in most places, so when he found a pretty Mediterranean house close to many of our friends I was thrilled.

Barry is a perfectionist who enjoys and appreciates the best of everything. He has exquisite taste in furnishings, so I left all of that to him. My only concern was how much he was spending. We were in the middle of our busiest travel season with Women of Faith, so I gave little thought to the appearance of a new chair or a different rug.

Until one day when I was faced with a reality that I had not anticipated.

That day I was expecting a check for work I had done over the period of a year. I had already talked with Barry about sending a portion to my mom and several others in mission work we have supported for some time.

But when the check arrived, my assistant told me the money was already spent.

She could tell that I was horrified, but this was just the tip of the iceberg. There was so much more that she had to tell me. I discovered that we were in substantial debt. I thought we had savings, but it was all gone. Barry felt such shame that he had asked my assistant not to tell me about our financial situation until he could work out what to do. I was confused, angry, and scared. When I asked him why he had let our finances get that bad without telling me, he had no answer. I asked my assistant to let me have everything on paper so that I could try to come up with some sort of plan. The stark facts in black and white were horrifying to me.

sinking

After that discovery, a rift began between Barry and me. I was trying to hold things together for Christian's sake, but I was struggling to make it through as well. I knew that I could not allow myself to slip into despair, but it was hard to hold everything together at home. We were in the middle of my busiest travel time with Women of Faith. For weeks, every Sunday when I flew home I would end up physically sick. I would have to throw up on the plane or pull over in the car as I got closer to the house. I didn't know what I was coming home to or what the atmosphere would be.

During those next few weeks and months, the rift between Barry and me became greater and greater. I tried to reach him, but it seemed as if he was living in a place where I couldn't go and was not welcome. Slowly but surely I began to withdraw from Barry emotionally. I moved into a self-preservation mode that only served to feed into his sense of hopelessness. I felt as if I was being torn in two. I wasn't sure what it would take to make Barry wake up to what was happening to our family or how long I could go on living as we were.

I finally gave Barry an ultimatum: he had to get help, or I was coming off the road. I couldn't continue pouring money into a bottomless pit and watch him disappear a little bit more each day. I think he finally began to grasp the weight of the situation. He made some inquiries and found a doctor in our area he could work with.

Unfortunately, by the time Barry grabbed hold of himself and began working intensely with a good Christian counselor, I was too tired to care anymore. He was doing everything he could to show real change, but I had erected a wall to protect myself and survive. I was exhausted and sick at heart. I don't believe I have ever felt so hopeless in my life. I could only share what was going on with a few trusted godly friends, and I was tired of trying to battle things through with Barry. But God was about to use a very dark night to remind me who my real enemy was.

that night

I had no idea hopelessness could feel so much like fear until that night. It had been a rough day. Barry and I had again discussed our current financial situation, which I found very stressful. It was hard for us to talk about it without me blaming him in my heart and him knowing it and feeling it deeply.

When Christian was finally asleep, I set about cleaning the kitchen. (One of the traits I have adopted from my mother is that I hate to wake up to a new day and have vestiges of the old still hanging around.) Once the dishes were loaded in the dishwasher and the counters cleaned, I sat for a while in the den flicking through television channels.

It's amazing to me that we have more than two hundred channels of nothing worth watching offered on a nightly basis. I tried all my favorites. BBC America was offering a show on race car drivers, so I passed on that. Discovery Channel had the guy who chooses to be abandoned in the wilderness and eats live snakes to survive, so I quickly passed on him. After a few more attempts, I gave up and turned the television off.

It was then I began to feel something.

I have struggled with depression for many years. What I was about to face that night was not this familiar foe but a presence that seemed to suck any warmth out of the room and out of my heart. It seemed to me—and as I write this, I have asked the Holy Spirit to help me remember with clarity—that the temperature in the room dropped several degrees in a matter of moments.

I have been a Christian since I was eleven years old. I have never dabbled with anything to do with the dark side and have had very little exposure to it that I am aware of. The only time that I have been acutely aware of evil was during a concert in Bangkok,

Thailand, when I was in my late twenties, but I had a team of prayer warriors holding me up in prayer backstage.

This was different. I felt the presence of evil in the room; I knew I was not alone. Barry had been in the bedroom, but at that moment he came in and asked me if I was coming to bed. I told him I wasn't ready yet, and then I asked him to do something I'm sure sounded very strange. I said, "Barry, I want you to go back to the bedroom and not come out until morning." Obviously he wasn't very comfortable with that, but I was very insistent.

For the next few hours, I felt as if I was in a very real battle for my life. The accuser told me I was alone. He told me there was no hope for us as a family. He said everything I cared about would be destroyed and there was absolutely nothing I could do about it. I fell to my knees on the floor and wept so bitterly I soaked part of the rug.

Then the softer voices started. The suggestion was clear and simple and given with no sound of malice. It was almost comforting.

There is a knife in the kitchen. You just dried it and put it away. If you take that knife and just brush it against your wrists, this will be over.

It won't hurt.

There will be no more pain.

You can do this. It is the best way for everyone.

It is amazing that Satan can make lies sound like truth. I am alert to voices that might scream in my face, but not always to those that whisper in my ear. For those few hours I experienced hopelessness and despair such as I have never faced before. I was so physically and emotionally exhausted that I had no strength left to fight.

You may ask, "Why didn't you call on the name of Jesus?" I did. It's all I *could* do. Every now and then, I would simply whisper his name as tears poured down my face and drenched the rug. For the duration of this dark visit, I felt as if I was being pulled further and further into a pit. I felt defeated.

But then, slowly, as I whispered Christ's name, I became aware of his presence. I knew with a certainty I have seldom felt that I had never really been alone at all.

I was on my face on the floor when it seemed to me that light had entered the room. I honestly believe that if I'd reached out my hand in that moment, I would have touched Jesus' feet. I felt as if his hand was stretched out to me to lift me up. His strength flowed into me.

I got on my knees, and then I finally was able to stand up. I turned to the forces of darkness and said just one word: "No!" Then I said it again with power, "In Jesus' name, no!" Then I went through to the bedroom and slept the rest of the night without distress.

In the morning everything was the same in the house, but something had changed in me. I recognized who my enemy had been all this time. I had been fighting the wrong person. Barry had made some bad choices, but he was not my enemy. It was Satan who wants nothing more than to tear apart everything that God loves most—his children.

For the next few days, I steeped myself in the Word of God. It was surprising to me that after forty years of walking with Christ I could forget what this life and this holy battle are all about. It is easy to fall into the world's definition of happiness and forget that we are only travelers on this planet. I was not put onto this earth to make myself happy. I was put here to learn to love and trust God and to let his love flow through me until we make it safely home.

Then God used our son to speak life into any residual darkness.

My main concern during this dark time was Christian. Barry and I both tried our best to protect him, but I know he felt the tension. One night I talked to him. I asked him what Dad or I could do to make life easier for him. I honestly expected him to say he wished Dad hadn't spent so much money because it had affected him, Christian, too. But he said nothing about Barry. Instead, what he said was about me.

He said, "I wish you weren't so angry at Dad."

"What do you mean?" I asked.

"Well, I know Dad did some things that weren't good, but you have to forgive him."

I was stunned. He said, "I don't want to hurt your feelings, Mom."

I told him I was very grateful for his honesty and he can always say what he feels. After he was asleep, I took the dogs for a long walk and poured out my feelings to God.

"This really stinks, God. Barry gets us into a mess, removes himself from the human race for two years, and I'm supposed to just let it all go and bake a pie?! That's just great. Thank you so much!"

My son's words burned in my heart. "*You have to forgive him.*" The truth is, I didn't want to forgive him. But Christian's words stayed with me.

i will deliver you

As I reflected on God's promise—*I will deliver you*—my question was, "Well, how will you do that?" I saw no sign of hope of getting out of the mess we were in.

But the more time I spent in my Father's presence, the more ridiculous my question was. It didn't matter *how*. All that mattered was *who*! If God my Father was telling me he would deliver me, then it didn't matter how or when. It was time for me to believe God can change any circumstance if we place our hope in him.

My Father's message to me was crystal clear:

Let go!

My cry had been, "Let go of what, Lord? I'm trying to hold on to our lives here. What do you want me to let go of?" It became clear to me that I was being invited to let go of everything.

- Let go of trying to fix this.
- Let go of trying to work out what will happen.
- Let go of protecting yourself.

I finally bowed my knee and let go. I released everything to God—my fear, my anger, my unforgiveness. I let go of all of that and clung to my Father's hand. A few weeks later, Barry and I celebrated our wedding anniversary. I asked Barry and Christian to join me in the den after supper. I had something I wanted to say.

"I want you both to know that tonight I am a very grateful woman," I told them. "I am thankful God loves and receives me just as I am. I am thankful I have a husband who loves me and has a heart open to change and to the love of God. I am thankful to have such an awesome son who speaks the truth even when it's hard. I am more thankful than I can say that God has his hand on us and will bring us through rough seas together because he loves us. I love you both so much."

delivered

The events, stories, quotes, and passages of Scripture you've read in this book have been God's tools to change my perspective of what deliverance should look like. I'm still paying off some bills, and life is not always easy or smooth, but what God has delivered me from is threefold:

He delivered me from hopelessness.

He delivered me from self-protection.

He delivered me from unforgiveness.

Satan would love to convince you right now that there is no hope in your situation. He would love to tell you to quit, just end it all, and it will be over with. That's all he has to offer. He has no good gifts, just despair and fear.

Hope is the resting place—the rock and the foundation—for all who have put their trust in Christ Jesus. When we surrender to him, we are at peace. When we give up our right to be right, we are at peace. When from the depths of our hearts we can tell God, "I trust you," heaven celebrates, hell shudders, and we are at peace.

That, my dear friend, is my prayer for you.

In the final chapter, I will share some of the things Barry and I did to strengthen our family, for it's our prayer that they will strengthen yours too.

deliverance discovered

1. In what ways have you experienced hopelessness in your life?
2. How do you combat despair?
3. What are you facing right now that you might have to reconsider who the real enemy in your situation is?
4. Where do you believe God is asking you to let go?

a prayer of deliverance

Father God,

Thank you for the body of Christ. Thank you that we can share our lives with one another and find hope in the midst of our hopelessness. Father, I confess now my areas of despair. . . .

I bring you every situation where I have lost hope and ask for your grace and your light and your peace. I bring you my family and ask for your protection and covering over our lives.

In Jesus' name, amen.

EIGHTEEN

the million-watt megabulb of God's hope

Do not look forward to the changes and chances of this life in fear; rather look to them with full hope that, as they arise, God, whose you are, will deliver you out of them. He is your Keeper. He has kept you hitherto. Hold fast to his dear hand, and he will lead you safely through all things; and, when you cannot stand, he will bear you in his arms. Do not look forward to what may happen tomorrow. Our Father will either shield you from suffering, or he will give you strength to bear it.

—Saint Francis de Sales

Through thick and thin, keep your hearts at attention, in adoration before Christ, your Master. Be ready to speak up and tell anyone who asks why you're living the way you are, and always with the utmost courtesy.

—1 Peter 3:15 msg

Hope is faith holding out its hands in the dark.

—George Iles

Therefore, having been justified by faith, we have peace with God through our Lord Jesus Christ, through whom also we have access by faith into this grace in which we stand, and rejoice in hope of the glory of God. And not only *that,* but we also glory in tribulations, knowing that tribulation produces perseverance; and perseverance, character; and character, hope. Now hope does not disappoint, because the love of God has been poured out in our hearts by the Holy Spirit who was given to us.

—Romans 5:1–5

"Where are you going?" her brother asked her as she headed out the door.

"I'm off to join the parade," she said. "Do you want to come?"

"What parade?" he asked.

"Trust me," she replied. "There is going to be a big, big parade."

"Well, who will be in it?" he asked.

"I don't know," she said. "I'll be in it."

"You already said that. Who else?"

"Why does that matter?" she replied. "It will be a wonderful parade. Come on!"

She strode out of the house, waving her flag in the air and singing. As she marched down the street, others joined her. From every home, boys and girls and moms and dads took their places and the sound of the parade got louder and louder. There were streamers and balloons of every shape and color. Some brought their musical instruments and added to the rhythm and the melody. Some were laughing, while others had tears of joy running down their cheeks. The song got louder and louder until it seemed to shake the very trees.

Make a joyful shout to God, all the earth!
Sing out the honor of His name;
Make His praise glorious.
Say to God,
"How awesome are Your works!
Through the greatness of Your power . . .
All the earth shall worship You
And sing praises to You;
They shall sing praises to Your name." (Psalm 66:1–4)

the dazzling light of hope

What is hope? Hope is only as strong as the object or person it is attached to. It has no value of its own. For example, I hope I can walk our dogs before the rain starts. I hope Christian is able to remember everything he studied for his science test. I have no control over these things. Sure, I could get up right now and take our dogs outside, but the rain might start before we get back. Christian studied and studied for his test last night, but he might have a bad day or a headache or any number of variables that could affect the outcome of his test.

This is not the hope we're looking at here. When we talk of the million-watt megabulb of God's hope, we are talking about something you and I can stake our very lives on. We are not talking about something we're crossing our fingers for or tucking our lucky rabbit's foot into our favorite Bible for. As I sit here today, one thing is crystal clear to me: my hope can be summed up in one name—*Jesus*!

If my hope is in anything else apart from Jesus, then it is too small. He is the answer to everything I need or anticipate. He is my deepest desire even when I don't immediately recognize that.

He is my yesterday, today, and tomorrow. When everything else fails, he will not. When everyone else fails, he will not. When I can't count on myself, I can count on him. When I'm not sure how to pay my bills, I can hope in him. When I don't know what's happening to our country, I can hope in him. When friends fail, he will not. When my health fails, he will not. When I disappoint others and myself, he will never disappoint. When I want to give up on myself, he will never give up on me. When I find it hard to love myself, he does not. When I have no grace for myself, he does. When I don't know what to do anymore, he does.

Do you see how securely your life is tucked into the very hand of the One who holds the universe in place? You are loved, you are loved, and, yes, you are loved!

building our hope on Christ

I want to share with you about what my family is building our hope on today. I cannot begin to tell you the changes I have seen in Barry. I admire his willingness to share part of his story in these pages; he did not have to do that. His desire to provide us with a beautiful home almost derailed us, but now he shows his care for Christian and me in small ways. Whether it's shooting hoops with Christian after school or putting in a load of laundry for me when I'm busy, his kindness touches our lives.

Kindness is underrated in our world. Simple acts of mercy leave more of the fragrance of Christ because they touch us where we live and where we are the thirstiest. Barry wrote me a note as I got close to finishing this book and asked me to include it.

> I never knew life could be so dark. I never believed depression and the brokenness that followed could or would ever happen to me. I

> knew there were places inside me that needed healing, and I knew that only God could heal them. At first, it was just grey. But then I began to sink deeper and deeper and it got darker and darker, even darker than I ever knew possible. Healing takes a long time. I learned that. Almost three years and I'm still going. But I am thankful that God loves me that much.
>
> He answered. He took *me* on. He let the pieces crumble right before my eyes. He watched the tears. He watched the pain. And maybe most importantly, He helped me let go. And with God, you don't just let go—you let go with abandon. I am learning to trust Him in a way I never knew possible. I will never be the same. Thank you for holding my hand as we watched Him put the pieces of a soul back together again.

I am touched and challenged by my husband's humility. I think it is particularly hard for a man to be this open and honest.

But is my hope for our family's future based on the evidence I see in Barry's life that he has changed? No, it's not. We are all vulnerable broken human beings who at any moment can fall. My hope is in the risen Christ, not in Barry.

When I look at my own life, is my hope that I will never cycle back into a deep well of depression again? No, my hope is in the risen Christ ruling and reigning in me.

As I look at our darling son, I see a boy who has a relationship with Jesus, who is smart and funny and athletic. But is my hope that he will never mess up? Absolutely not. My hope is in the grace and mercy of our redemptive God, who watches over his sheep.

If I place my hope in anything or anyone other than Jesus, I will be disappointed. When we expect others to be what only Jesus can be, we set them and ourselves up for heartache. If my hope is that the economy will improve, the housing market will improve, or my own finances will improve, then I have placed my hope on a shaky foundation.

a foundation of rock or sand?

When Jesus told the parable about building your house on a sure foundation, his words were very direct. Sometimes we miss the impact of the parables and chalk them up as merely nice stories to tell children in Sunday school. That's not the case. Jesus chose his words very carefully, and each of his stories can have a profound lesson if you're open to it. If you read the following passage carefully, it is life changing.

> These words I speak to you are not incidental additions to your life, homeowner improvements to your standard of living. They are foundational words, words to build a life on. If you work these words into your life, you are like a smart carpenter who built his house on solid rock. Rain poured down, the river flooded, a tornado hit—but nothing moved that house. It was fixed to the rock. But if you just use my words in Bible studies and don't work them into your life, you are like a stupid carpenter who built his house on the sandy beach. When a storm rolled in and the waves came up, it collapsed like a house of cards. (Matthew 7:24–26 MSG)

This passage comes at the end of what we know as the Sermon on the Mount contained in Matthew 5–7. The illustration of what happens when you build your life on a foundation that is less than secure would have had great significance to Jesus' audience. Palestine was known for torrential rains that could turn a dry riverbed into a raging torrent in a matter of moments. Only the extreme weather revealed the quality of the building. Two homes could look exactly the same until the weather changed and only the one built on a solid foundation would survive. Even as Jesus was telling the story, people would be able to see in their mind's eye homes that they had witnessed being washed away.

The response at the end of his talk was the equivalent of our standing ovation:

> When Jesus concluded his address, the crowd burst into applause. They had never heard teaching like this. It was apparent that he was living everything he was saying—quite a contrast to their religion teachers! This was the best teaching they had ever heard. (Matthew 7:28–29 MSG)

I wonder how many from the crowd that day went away and applied what Jesus said. It is one thing to be stirred by a great message; it's quite another to live it.

I also wonder how many of us would go away and apply what Jesus said, if we were privileged enough to hear his message. Just as with Jesus' listeners, it's an applicable lesson. We are living, as they were then, in a world where many people build their lives on sand—whether intentionally or not.

Our son is blessed to attend a Christian school. I am grateful for that, as his instructors endeavor to teach all of life from a sacred perspective. But even there, many families are crumbling. The school found it necessary this year to start a divorce support group for the elementary school children.

If that is your situation as you read this book—divorce or any other life-altering event—my heart goes out to you more than I can put into words. No one would choose that. No one wants to have their lives ripped apart or see their children having to make choices children should not have to make. But as Jesus said, such events are the ones that reveal the foundation of our faith. Only the devastation of storms will reveal the integrity of the structure.

Which is where our million-watt megabulb of hope comes in. Is it only for those who appear to have their ducks in a row? Can it only be claimed by those who think they have made good choices all along the line? A thousand times, no! It is for those who need a Savior. It is for the broken and the wounded—the foundationally challenged. It is for you and for me.

if your cheese keeps falling off your cracker . . .

Tucked in the introduction to Brennan Manning's book *The Ragamuffin Gospel* is a great statement. He wrote that his book is not for those who have their lives neatly in order but for people like you and me "whose cheese keeps falling off their crackers."[1] It's for the homeschool mom, the working woman, and the single mother trying to make enough to feed her child. When God looks down on our world, his eyes see what we don't see. He sees his beloved children lost and struggling to make sense out of things that make no sense. We all search for meaning and purpose, but there is no lasting meaning and purpose apart from Jesus.

No matter the circumstance of your life at this moment, you can choose right here and now to place all your hope for today and tomorrow, for your family and your health, for your finances and your future, in Christ and in Christ alone. The glory of this is that no one in heaven or on earth or under the earth can touch that hope. We know that we can be messed with in this life. Your health might be bad at the moment, or you may be struggling with finances, rebelling children, or a difficult marriage. But your hope in Christ stands, solid as the Rock that he is.

on Christ the solid rock i stand

Edward Mote wrote the marvelous hymn "The Solid Rock" in 1834. He started with just two lines:

On Christ the solid Rock I stand
All other ground is sinking sand.

When Edward got home from church, he began to work on the verses. The following Sunday, one of his best friends told him that his wife's illness had taken a critical turn and she was dying. He asked Edward if he would come home with him and pray with his wife.

When they arrived, his friend's wife asked if they might sing a hymn. Her husband looked for their hymnbook, which was always kept by her bed, but he couldn't find it. So Edward asked if he might share something he had just written. This is what he sang that day to her as she passed from this life into Jesus' arms:

My hope is built on nothing less
Than Jesus' blood and righteousness.
I dare not trust the sweetest frame,
But wholly trust in Jesus' Name.

On Christ the solid Rock I stand,
All other ground is sinking sand;
All other ground is sinking sand.

When darkness seems to hide His face,
I rest on His unchanging grace.
In every high and stormy gale,
My anchor holds within the veil.

His oath, His covenant, His blood,
Support me in the whelming flood.
When all around my soul gives way,
He then is all my Hope and Stay.

When He shall come with trumpet sound,
Oh may I then in Him be found.
Dressed in His righteousness alone,
Faultless to stand before the throne.

On Christ the solid Rock I stand,
All other ground is sinking sand;
All other ground is sinking sand.[2]

the great irony

The great irony of the Christian life is that the cross, which looked to be an end, is our beginning. What looked like a sealed chamber became an open door. I have found that to be true in my own life—when I come to the end of myself, I find in Christ a new beginning.

Human hope looks for all things to be well on this earth, and yet we know—or need to know—that will never happen. Hope that is built on Christ accepts there may be many small deaths on this earth but understands they all lead to our real life, which is hidden with God in Christ Jesus. There have been many great books, beautiful paintings, and glorious sculptures on the love of God, each portraying a tiny piece of the whole. But none will compare with when we see Jesus face-to-face: "Now we see through a glass, darkly," but then we shall see face-to-face (1 Corinthians 13:12 KJV)!

I realize today in a way and at a depth I never have before that we are in a spiritual battle. We forget that at our own peril. The enemy wants to destroy our lives and destroy our families, and the greatest battle of all is in the mind. When the apostle Paul wrote to the church in Corinth, he warned them that what they see with their eyes is not all they are wrestling with:

> For though we walk in the flesh, we do not war according to the flesh. For the weapons of our warfare are not carnal but mighty in God for pulling down strongholds, casting down arguments and every high thing that exalts itself against the knowledge of God, bringing every thought into captivity to the obedience of Christ. (2 Corinthians 10:3–5)

We do not need to defeat the devil; Jesus has already done that. We just need to believe it and live in it. You don't have to out-yell Satan. You just have to out-truth him! He is a defeated enemy.

barry's prayer

If you were to ask Barry today what things helped him find hope again, he would tell you that coming to the end of himself brought him face-to-face with Jesus at a depth he had never experienced before. He would also share with you a prayer that he prays every single day without exception. It is from Richard Foster's book *Prayer*. Let me share it with you as we close:

> In the strong name of Jesus Christ, I stand against the world, the flesh, and the devil. I resist every force that would seek to distract me from my center in God. I reject the distorted concepts and ideas that would make sin plausible and desirable. I oppose every attempt to keep me from knowing full fellowship with God.
>
> By the power of the Holy Spirit I speak directly to the thoughts,

emotions, and desires of my heart and command you to find your satisfaction in the infinite variety of God's love rather than the bland diet of sin. I call upon the good, the true, and the beautiful to rise up within me and the evil to subside. I ask for an increase of righteousness, peace, and joy in the Holy Spirit.

By the authority of almighty God, I tear down Satan's strongholds in my life, in the lives of those I love, and in the society in which I live. I take into myself the weapons of truth, righteousness, peace, salvation, the word of God, and prayer. I command every evil influence to leave; you have no right here and I allow you no point of entry. I ask for an increase of faith, hope, and love so that, by the power of God, I can be a light set on a hill, causing truth and justice to flourish.

These things I pray for the sake of him who loved me and gave himself for me. Amen.[3]

deliverance discovered

1. How would you define hope now?
2. In what areas in your life do you need a more solid foundation?
3. How will you intentionally take every thought captive?
4. What new practices can you add to your life to foster hope?
5. Write a prayer for your family.

a prayer of deliverance

Dear Father,

By the authority of almighty God, I tear down Satan's strongholds in my life, in the lives of those I love, and in the society in which I live. I take into myself the weapons of truth, righteousness, peace, salvation, the Word of God, and prayer. I command every evil influence to leave; they have no right here and I allow them no point of entry. I ask for an increase of faith, hope, and love so that, by the power of God, I can be a light set on a hill, causing truth and justice to flourish.

These things I pray for the sake of him who loved me and gave himself for me.

In Jesus' name, amen.

CONCLUSION

a long-awaited deliverance

Have you ever prayed for something for so long that you wonder if there will be an answer this side of heaven? I have. It broke my heart and sometimes invaded my dreams and my sleep. Then, when I least expected it, there it was. I had no idea God could put so much beauty into tragedy.

a haunting question

Christian and I took our trip to Scotland in 2007 for reasons that made sense to me. I wanted to see my mom and thought it would be fun to have a mother-and-son trip together after the rough couple of years our family had been through. I had no idea God had planned something so life-changing for me.

I told you earlier that on the day I took my mom to the hospital to get new batteries for her hearing aid, I suddenly found myself parked in front of the psychiatric hospital where my father died. It was a shock to me. I have always hated that place, for to me it is a place of nightmares.

What I didn't tell you was that the next day, I went back—

alone. All I knew from my mom was that my father had escaped from the hospital one night. They searched and searched for him and found him dead the next morning, caught in the salmon nets in the river behind the hospital.

I had nightmares about my father's death. The thing that horrified me was wondering what happened to my dad in those last few moments. Did he slip and fall into the river? Was he in such despair that he could no longer go on? Did he feel as if he was all alone?

That was the worst question for me: had my dad felt as if all on earth and all in heaven had abandoned him?

i'm going to take the walk

When I went back alone the next day it was for one purpose. I wanted to take the walk I believed my father must have taken. It took me a few minutes to get from the hospital to the river's edge. As I stood there, I found myself asking, "Is this the last place where your feet touched this earth, Dad? . . . Did you feel as if you were all alone?"

I wish I had the gift to be able to express adequately to you what happened to me in that moment. As I stood there, it was like a scene change in a movie. I was no longer a little girl wondering why her daddy had left her. I was a fifty-one-year-old woman looking at the last place her thirty-four-year-old father had touched this earth. As I stood there, expecting to be engulfed in sorrow, I was met instead by Jesus. He stood beside me and said, *I was there. He wasn't alone. He went from this grassy bank into my arms. He wasn't alone for even a moment.*

I went down on my knees, and this place of nightmares became holy ground. All I could think of was the hymn my dad was known for: "There Were Ninety and Nine." My dad had a wonderful voice, and this had been one of his favorite hymns to sing. As I knelt by the banks of the river that day, I believe Jesus said to me, *Sheila, on that day I sang it back to him.*

There were ninety and nine that safely lay
In the shelter of the fold.
But one was out on the hills away,
Far off from the gates of gold.
Away on the mountains wild and bare.
Away from the tender Shepherd's care.
Away from the tender Shepherd's care.

But none of the ransomed ever knew
How deep were the waters crossed;
Nor how dark was the night the Lord passed through
Ere He found His sheep that was lost.
Out in the desert He heard its cry,
Sick and helpless and ready to die;
Sick and helpless and ready to die.

And all through the mountains, thunder riven
And up from the rocky steep,
There arose a glad cry to the gate of Heaven,
"Rejoice! I have found My sheep!"
And the angels echoed around the throne,
"Rejoice, for the Lord brings back His own!
Rejoice, for the Lord brings back His own!"[1]

So that is my story. I find that life is a curious blending of joy and sorrow, mystery and moments of recognition. As I sit here, finishing this book, I am thinking about you. Your story is different from mine. You have walked through things I can't even imagine. But here is one constant factor, one resounding truth: we are loved, we are loved, we are loved by God.

Is being loved enough to help you "let go"? For me it is. Being loved by the divine architect of everything that matters is enough. I don't know what tomorrow holds, but that's okay. God does. I don't know what tomorrow holds for you or those who matter to you, but God does. This is not a small piece of information; it is life-changing stuff. Sometimes we have to wait for years for answers. Sometimes we wait a whole lifetime. But trust me, ladies: *this ends well for us!*

> No one's ever seen or heard anything like this,
> Never so much as imagined anything quite like it—
> What God has arranged for those who love him.
> (1 Corinthians 2:9 MSG)

deliverance: the power of a word

The deliverance we are promised in Christ does not fall under the heading of "wishful thinking." Throughout the Word of God, we have a record of God's faithfulness to his people over and over again. Even as they vacillated back and forth, God stood firm. Their faithlessness did not eradicate his faithfulness.

We live in a world that bombards us with information every second of the day. Some of the information is accurate, but more often than not, particularly if someone is trying to sell us something, the information is not trustworthy.

By contrast, God's Word is 100 percent trustworthy. As we look at areas of our lives where we long to know God's freedom and deliverance, you may feel you have tried my suggestions before and failed. What I long for you to see is that we are not asked to deliver ourselves. That is God's job. We are simply asked to let go of the things that are hurting us but that we still cling to. God has promised to deliver us.

The word *deliver* is a powerful declaration of the passionate commitment of God to save his people. Looking at the original meaning of the word, as used in the Psalms or in the words of Jesus or the apostle Paul, helps us understand the depth and breadth of what we believe and also helps us understand how to pray.

Psalm 72:11–12 is a psalm of King Solomon. In it, he declared:

> Yes, all kings shall fall down before Him;
> All nations shall serve Him.
> For He will *deliver* the needy when he cries,
> The poor also, and him who has no helper. (emphasis added)

The word used here for "deliver" is the Hebrew word *natsal*, meaning "to recover, to rescue."

In Psalm 50, we find another Hebrew word used for *deliver*:

> Call upon Me in the day of trouble;
> I will *deliver* you, and you shall glorify Me. (v. 15; emphasis added)

In this passage, the Hebrew word used for "deliver" is *chalats*, which means "to strengthen."

What wonderful promises! Not only will God rescue and recover us when we put our trust in him, but he will also strengthen us.

Likewise the Lord's Prayer, found in Matthew 6, is brought to a powerful conclusion by Christ's confident prayer for deliverance:

> Our Father in heaven, may your name be honored.
> May your kingdom come soon.
> May your will be done here on earth, just as it is in heaven.
> Give us our food for today, and forgive us our sins,
> just as we have forgiven those who have sinned against us.
> And don't let us yield to temptation, but *deliver* us
> from the evil one. (vv. 9–13 NLT; emphasis added)

The Greek word here for "deliver" is *rhuomai*. It's a strong word meaning "to draw out with force and violence, to drag out of danger." The same word is used in Luke 1: "We have been *rescued* from our enemies, so we can serve God without fear, in holiness and righteousness forever" (vv. 74–75 NLT; emphasis added).

This particular use of *delivered* is also part of the prophecy of Zacharias. You may remember that Zacharias's wife, Elizabeth, was the cousin of Mary, the mother of Jesus. The angel Gabriel appeared to Zacharias and told him that his wife was going to have a son and they should name him John. Zacharias was very skeptical, as his wife was well past her child-bearing years. Gabriel was insulted by his questioning. He told Zacharias that he stood in the very presence of God and that because of his doubt he would be unable to speak until the moment the baby was born. When Elizabeth finally gave birth, Zacharias wrote on a tablet that the baby was to be named John.

In Paul's letter to the church in Rome, we find the passage where Paul laid out the dilemma of every believer: *Why do I do the things I don't want to do and don't do the very things I want to do?* "O wretched man that I am! Who will *deliver* me from this body of death?" (7:24; emphasis added). In other words, who will *rhuomai* me, drag me, with great force pull me from this miserable place?

He answered his own question with this glorious declaration: "I thank God—through Jesus Christ our Lord" (7:25). In this verse, Paul expressed the heartfelt cry of every believer at some point in his or her life. Which one of us has not struggled in some area of our lives and felt so desperate that it would take the drastic intervention of God to pull us free?

We may have assigned the word *delivered* to the realm of the pizza boy, but when God tells us that he will deliver us it is a powerful promise. He will rescue and strengthen us. With the full power of God he will wrench us from the grip of our enemies. We have an advocate and defender like no other. Praise be to God!

NOTES

one: Fresh-Baked Grace for the Spiritually Hungry

1. Charles Finney, quoted in Edythe Draper, *Draper's Book of Quotations for the Christian World* (Wheaton, IL: Tyndale, 1992).
2. Martin Luther, quoted in Edythe Draper, *Draper's Book of Quotations for the Christian World* (Wheaton, IL: Tyndale, 1992).

two: This Dead Religion Is Past Its Sell-By Date

1. Chuck Swindoll, *The Grace Awakening* (Dallas: Word, 1990); Lewis Smedes, *Shame and Grace: Healing the Shame We Don't Deserve* (New York: HarperOne, 1994).

three: Living in the Past

1. Alice Miller, *The Drama of the Gifted Child: The Search for the True Self* (New York: Basic Books, 1994).

four: Look at the View Ahead!

1. Dr. Herbert Lockyer, *Every Woman of the Bible* (Grand Rapids: Zondervan, 1967), 130.

five: The Trap of Unforgiveness

1. J. A. Blumenthal, W. Jiang, M. A. Babyak, D. S. Krantz, D. J. Frid, R. E. Coleman, R. Waugh, M. Hanson, M. Appelbaum, C. O'Connor and J. J. Morris, *Archives of Internal Medicine* (October 27, 1997): 157.

six: Don't Play Fair—It Will Set You Free

1. Lewis B. Smedes, *The Art of Forgiving* (Nashville: Moorings, 1996); emphasis in original.

seven: The Trouble with Temptation Is That It's Just So Tempting

1. *Adam Clarke's Commentary on the New Testament,* notes on Matthew 4. Electronic Edition STEP Files Copyright © 2005, QuickVerse. All rights reserved.
2. Josephus, (Antiquities l. xv. c. 14).

eight: Let Go and Live in Christ's Victory

1. Corrie ten Boom, quoted in Edythe Draper, *Draper's Book of Quotations for the Christian World* (Wheaton, IL: Tyndale, 1992).

nine: Shame on You!

1. Lewis Smedes, *Shame and Grace: Healing the Shame We Don't Deserve* (New York: HarperOne, 1994).

fourteen: God Will Prove It's a Love Story

1. *The Expositor's Bible Commentary*, vol. 2 (Grand Rapids: Zondervan, 1990).
2. Oswald Chambers, quoted in Edythe Draper, *Draper's Book of Quotations for the Christian World* (Wheaton, IL: Tyndale, 1992).
3. Thomas Merton, quoted in Edythe Draper, *Draper's Book of Quotations for the Christian World* (Wheaton, IL: Tyndale, 1992).
4. "The Love of God," words by Frederick M. Lehman, 1917.

fifteen: We Are What We Believe We Are?

1. Herman Hesse, quoted in Edythe Draper, *Draper's Book of Quotations for the Christian World* (Wheaton, IL: Tyndale, 1992).
2. William Shakespeare, *Hamlet*, III.ii.
3. James Burtchaell, *Philemon's Problem* (Grand Rapids: Eerdmans; Jubilee edition, 1998).

sixteen: Table for Two, Please

1. Louie Giglio, YouTube sermon excerpt, http://www.youtube.com/watch?v=_e4zgJXPpI4; accessed August 9, 2008.

eighteen: The Million-Watt Megabulb of God's Hope

1. Brennan Manning, *The Ragamuffin Gospel* (Sisters, OR: Multnomah, 2005).
2. Edward Mote, "My Hope Is Built: The Solid Rock," Cyber Hymnal, http://www.cyberhymnal.org/htm/m/y/myhopeis.htm; accessed August 9, 2008.
3. Richard Foster, *Prayer* (NY: Harper Collins).

Conclusion

1. "There Were Ninety and Nine," words by Elizabeth C. Clephane, 1868.

STUDY GUIDE

Chapter One
Fresh-baked Grace for the Spiritually Hungry

FIND

Here it is in a nutshell: Just as one person did it wrong and got us in all this trouble with sin and death, another person did it right and got us out of it. But more than just getting us out of trouble, he got us into life! One man said no to God and put many people in the wrong; one man said yes to God and put many in the right. All that passing laws against sin did was produce more lawbreakers. But sin didn't, and doesn't, have a chance in competition with the aggressive forgiveness we call grace. When it's sin versus grace, grace wins hands down. (Romans 5:18-20 MSG)

1. In what ways have you experienced God's aggressive forgiveness?
2. What are you dealing with right now that you don't remember signing up for?
3. How do you know God is in control of the situation described above?

FEEL

1. How do you feel when God challenges you to let go of your agenda?
2. What are some of the things that happen in your daily life that have the potential to rob you of your peace and joy?
3. What can you do to guard yourself against those intruders? What is the role of God's grace in your response to life's challenges?

FOLLOW

1. How would you rate your spiritual hunger?
   __ I'm not hungry right now.
   __ I just need a snack.
   __ I'm on a diet.
   __ I'm starving.

2. How does your spiritual hunger affect your attitude toward the people God brings into your life?
3. Do you believe—not just in your head but deep in your soul—that God loves you as you are right now? Explain.
4. Write a prayer expressing your desires. Throughout the coming week, use this prayer as part of your conversation with God.

Chapter Two
This Dead Religion Is Past Its Sell-By Date

FIND

This only I want to learn from you: Did you receive the Spirit by the works of the law, or by the hearing of faith? Are you so foolish?

Having begun in the Spirit, are you now being made perfect by the flesh? Have you suffered so many things in vain—if indeed it was in vain? (Galatians 3:2-4)

1. Read the passage above. In your own words, what was Paul saying to the believers in Galatia?
2. Do you want to be seen for who you really are? Why or why not?
3. What are some of the dangers associated with being totally honest and vulnerable to others? With whom would you most likely be totally honest about your feelings and thoughts?

FEEL

1. Describe a time when you were judgmental of another person. How do you think that person would have felt if she had known your thoughts?
2. How do you feel when others hold you to a standard they cannot or will not live up to?
3. Read Matthew 22:34-40. How would someone who is a legalist view Jesus' summary of the basic principles of the Law?

FOLLOW

1. How would you describe the freshness of your faith?
   __ It is fresh-baked everyday.
   __ It is day-old but usable.
   __ It is dry, stale, and crusty.

2. What should be your daily routine for restoring the freshness of your faith?

3. What do you believe is the difference between accountability and legalism?
4. Write a prayer expressing your desires. Throughout the coming week, use this prayer as part of your conversation with God.

Chapter Three
Living in the Past

FIND

Forget about what's happened; don't keep going over old history. Be alert, be present. I'm about to do something brand-new. It's bursting out! Don't you see it? There it is! I'm making a road through the desert, rivers in the badlands. (Isaiah 43:18-19 MSG)

1. What is God's attitude toward your past?
2. Based on God's attitude, what should be your attitude toward your past?
3. What keeps you from letting God do something new in and through your life?

FEEL

1. How do you respond to your feelings of negativity? Do you give into the past, or do you use the past to understand your future in Christ? Explain.
2. What experiences or wounds in your past might God use to comfort another believer?
3. What effect is your past having on your personal and spiritual health?

FOLLOW

1. Do you spend more time focused on what is true or on what you wish were true? Explain how this affects your attitudes and actions.
2. Read 1 Peter 5:8. How is your past being used against you?
3. Based on the truth of God's Word, how will you respond to Satan's lies about your past?
4. Write a prayer expressing your desires. Throughout the coming week, use this prayer as part of your conversation with God.

Chapter Four
Look at the View Ahead!

FIND

I'm not saying that I have this all together, that I have it made. But I am well on my way, reaching out for Christ, who has so wondrously reached out for me. Friends, don't get me wrong: By no means do I count myself an expert in all of this, but I've got my eye on the goal, where God is beckoning us onward—to Jesus. I'm off and running, and I'm not turning back. (Philippians 3:12-14 MSG)

1. Read the passage above. Rewrite the passage in your own words expressing your determination to move ahead with God.
2. "How we view ourselves determines how far we believe we can progress on this spiritual journey" (p. 41). What is your reaction to this statement?
3. Think back to the moment when you first met Jesus Christ. How has your life changed since then?

FEEL

1. The Bible is full of stories in which God forgave someone's past and blessed his or her future. If God did this back then, He can do it today. How do you feel knowing that God is willing to forgive your past and bless your future?
2. On the line below, place an X marking the focus of your life.

   ←——————————————————————→

   Rearview mirror   Straight ahead

   What will happen if you try to move forward while looking backwards?
3. How would your life be different if you were freed from the bondage of your past?

FOLLOW

1. What events or disappointments in your past are holding you back?
2. Do you believe God is watching over you at all times? Explain your response.
3. Write a prayer expressing your desires. Throughout the coming week, use this prayer as part of your conversation with God.

Chapter Five
The Trap of Unforgiveness

FIND

Our Father in heaven,
Hallowed be Your name.
Your kingdom come.
Your will be done
On earth as it is in heaven.
Give us this day our daily bread.
And forgive us our debts,
As we forgive our debtors.
And do not lead us into temptation,
But deliver us from the evil one. (Matthew 6:9-13)

1. You've probably heard the prayer above many times. Take a moment and review each statement. Beside each statement, write a few words detailing how the prayer relates to your life right now.
2. What is the connection between God's forgiveness of us and our forgiveness of others? If God forgave you like you forgive others, what would be your standing before God?
3. How do anger and bitterness affect you emotionally, physically, and spiritually? What do you hope to accomplish through your anger and bitterness?

FEEL

1. Why is it so hard to forgive people?
2. What risks are you taking when you offer unconditional forgiveness?

3. Review the risks you listed and mark the ones that are most troubling to you.
4. Describe a time when you took your pain to Christ and He delivered healing. How did that make you feel?

FOLLOW

1. How can letting go of your hurts help you grow closer to God?
2. Who has wounded your heart? How can your relationship with God help you recover from the pain you experienced?
3. Write a prayer expressing your desires. Throughout the coming week, use this prayer as part of your conversation with God.

Chapter Six
Don't Play Fair—It Will Set You Free

FIND

I, even I, am He who blots out your transgressions for My own sake; And I will not remember your sins. (Isaiah 43:25)

1. Why would God want to blot out our sins? What's in it for Him?
2. Because God wants to be in a relationship with us, what should be our attitude toward ourselves?
3. How does regret affect your daily life? Read John 8:32. What truth do you need to know, and what freedom will you experience upon knowing it?

FEEL

1. Why is it sometimes hard to accept forgiveness?
2. "Forgiveness means being comfortable with ourselves, the good and the bad. We don't have to be perfect" (p. 71). What does that statement mean to you?
3. When you are truly able to forgive yourself, you'll be able to live with yourself. In what areas of life do you need to forgive yourself?

FOLLOW

1. How does the story of Paul's conversion impact your understanding of forgiveness?
2. In what ways do you separate guilt and shame in your own life?
3. As you think about your future, what strength can you gain from the knowledge of God's total forgiveness?
4. Since God has forgiven you, what assignment are you unqualified for?
5. Write a prayer expressing your desires. Throughout the coming week, use this prayer as part of your conversation with God.

Chapter Seven
The Trouble with Temptation Is That It's Just So Tempting

FIND

No test or temptation that comes your way is beyond the course of what others have had to face. All you need to remember is that God will never let you down; he'll never let you be pushed past your limit; he'll always be there to help you come through it. (1 Corinthians 10:13 MSG)

1. Read the verse above. What are the primary sources of your temptations?
2. How does your desire for immediate gratification affect your response to temptation?
3. "A person preoccupied with herself is a person not preoccupied with God" (p. 77). With what are you most often preoccupied?

FEEL

1. Jesus was tempted through some very natural desires. His resistance was rooted in His knowledge of Scripture. If your ability to resist temptation is dependent upon your knowledge of Scripture, how much danger are you in?
2. What do you really need to feel better about yourself? How does your response compare to God's thoughts about you?
3. Have you ever been tempted to take an easier path than the one you believe would honor God? Explain your response.

FOLLOW

1. Satan tempted Jesus to show off. In what ways are you tempted to call attention to yourself? What is God's attitude toward your behavior?
2. Miracles don't change hearts. Obedience does. In what areas of life do you need to be more obedient to God's expectations and principles?
3. In what places in your life or the life of your family does it seem that you might have compromised?
4. What will be the effect on your family of your uncompromising obedience to God?

5. Write a prayer expressing your desires. Throughout the coming week, use this prayer as part of your conversation with God.

Chapter Eight
Let Go and Live in Christ's Victory

FIND

So here's what I want you to do, God helping you: Take your everyday, ordinary life—your sleeping, eating, going-to-work, and walking-around life—and place it before God as an offering. Embracing what God does for you is the best thing you can do for him. (Romans 12:1 MSG)

1. The verse above mentions sleeping, eating, going-to-work, and walking-around as ways for you to honor God. Which of these areas of life is most difficult for you to relinquish to God? Why?
2. "Christ paid with everything he had so that you and I could be delivered from the things that hold us captive" (p 90). What things are holding you captive? How would your life change if you were set free from them?
3. When we focus on God, Satan's schemes become more obvious. What are three things you do daily to focus your life on God?

FEEL

1. How do you feel when you doubt God's control over a situation or His love for you?
2. Describe a time when God tested you. What did you learn about God and yourself through that situation?

FOLLOW

1. God wants us to embrace and rest in what he has done for us. Yet sometimes we want to try too hard to be something we're not. What would change in your life if you simply rested in God's love for you?
2. Satan causes us to fear certain situations. Some areas of life in which we experience fear are finances, energy, diet, parenting, and relationships. Which of these areas causes you the greatest fear? What happens to your motivation to please God when fear moves into your life?
3. Read Philippians 4:6-7. What is God saying to you through those verses?
4. In what areas of your life are you being invited to pull your will in line with the will of God?
5. Write a prayer expressing your desires. Throughout the coming week, use this prayer as part of your conversation with God.

Chapter Nine
Shame on You!

FIND

The religion scholars and Pharisees led in a woman who had been caught in an act of adultery. They stood her in plain sight of everyone and said, "Teacher, this woman was caught red-handed in the act of adultery. (John 8:3-4 MSG)

1. Shame is "the dead weight of not-good-enough-ness" (p. 102). Describe a time when you have felt shame.
2. The woman caught in adultery had committed a crime that was worthy of death. If you received the punishment

for your sins, what would you receive? How has God's grace changed that situation?

3. One of the scariest things to do is to express our problems. What problems are you facing alone right now?
4. Do you believe God wants to rid you of the weight of that problem? Why or why not?

FEEL

1. We often don't deal with an issue until we are desperate. Desperation overcomes the shame that we might feel. How desperate are you for freedom from life's struggles?
2. Shame sometimes keeps us from exercising our faith. We fail to speak up, we don't share our concerns, and we isolate ourselves from people who can help us through whatever it is we are facing. How would you characterize your transparency with other believers?
   __ like a brick wall
   __ like a window with shades
   __ like a door that opens and closes
   __ like clear glass

3. How does it make you feel knowing that God says you are beautiful, loved, and worth loving?

FOLLOW

1. The Bible is full of stories in which people who were outcasts in society were used as incredible tools for His purposes. If all of the resistance was gone, what might God do through your life?
2. What ministry might God establish through your story of redemption and forgiveness?

3. Write your testimony. Keep it short and simple. Don't try to tell everything, just tell the story so God is glorified.
4. Write a prayer expressing your desires. Throughout the coming week, use this prayer as part of your conversation with God.

Chapter Ten
Shame on Him

FIND

He is despised and rejected by men,
A Man of sorrows and acquainted with grief.
And we hid, as it were, our faces from Him;
He was despised, and we did not esteem Him.
Surely He has borne our griefs
And carried our sorrows;
Yet we esteemed Him stricken,
Smitten by God, and afflicted.
But He was wounded for our transgressions,
He was bruised for our iniquities;
The chastisement for our peace was upon Him,
And by His stripes we are healed. (Isaiah 53:3-5)

1. Read Hebrews 9:13-14. What was Christ's role in our redemption? In what ways was He the scapegoat?
2. Jesus got what He didn't deserve so you and I would not get what we do deserve. Write a few sentences expressing your thankfulness to God for this truth.
3. God didn't have to send Jesus as a sacrifice for us. He did it because He loves us. How often do you think

about the depth of God's love? What difference does it make when you do think about it?

FEEL

1. While on the cross, Jesus experienced momentary separation from God. His aloneness was severe. How do you know you won't experience permanent separation from God when you die?
2. Jesus carried our shame so we no longer have to carry it. We are free from the curse because he became a curse for us. How does that make you feel?
3. Have you ever felt forsaken? What caused that feeling?

FOLLOW

1. What would happen in your life if you let Jesus take away your sorrow and set you free?
2. How are you affected by secret sins?
3. Write a prayer giving Jesus authority over your secret sin.
4. To be loved like God loves us demands a response. What is your response to God's unconditional and never-ending love?
5. Write a prayer expressing your desires. Throughout the coming week, use this prayer as part of your conversation with God.

Chapter Eleven
You Are You for a Reason

FIND

After rising from the dead, Jesus appeared early on Sunday morning to Mary Magdalene, whom he had delivered from seven demons.

She went to his former companions, now weeping and carrying on, and told them. When they heard her report that she had seen him alive and well, they didn't believe her. (Mark 16:9-11 MSG)

1. Mary's experience with Jesus was the main point of her testimony. If you shared with someone what Jesus is doing in your life right now, what would you share?
2. When you find yourself in a contemplative state, do you ever wish you were someone else? Why or why not?
3. If you could change one thing about your life, what would it be and why?

FEEL

1. How do you feel about life in general? Are you optimistic and positive or pessimistic and negative? Why?
2. What limitations do you face every day? How do you move beyond your limitations to become the person God intended you to be?
3. Who are the people God has placed in your life who are sources of encouragement and support for you?

FOLLOW

1. Read Psalm 139:13-16. How does that psalm make you feel about yourself and God's involvement in your life?
2. God knew everything about you before you ever breathed your first breath, and He loves you. How can you reflect God's love for you toward people who doubt His love for them?
3. In what ways do you tend to judge your worth by your circumstances?

4. Is there something about your life that you think is an accident? Explain.
5. Write a prayer asking God to help you see yourself the way He sees you.
6. Write a prayer expressing your desires. Throughout the coming week, use this prayer as part of your conversation with God.

Chapter Twelve
I Was Made for This

FIND

I'm no longer calling you servants because servants don't understand what their master is thinking and planning. No, I've named you friends because I've let you in on everything I've heard from the Father. You didn't choose me, remember; I chose you, and put you in the world to bear fruit, fruit that won't spoil. (John 15:15-16 MSG)

1. Based on the passage above, would Jesus call you a servant or a friend? Why?
2. You were chosen by God for a purpose. For what do you think you were chosen?
3. We can easily believe that God left us here for our own pleasure. However, we were left here to make Him famous. In what ways are you making God famous in your daily life?

FEEL

1. How does it make you feel knowing that God left you here to make Himself famous?

2. Think about your life from God's perspective. How do you think He feels about your life? Is He proud, disappointed, angry? Explain your response.
3. Even though you don't always feel like a princess, you are still God's princess. How can that truth change the way you approach every day?

FOLLOW

1. On what are you relying to reach your greatest potential?
2. What is God's role in your life plan?
3. Have you ever felt as if your life doesn't matter much? How did that feeling affect your daily life?
4. Is God's calling in your life ever confusing? What do you want to ask God?
5. Use the space below to write a prayer asking God to help you see yourself the way He sees you.
6. Write a prayer expressing your desires. Throughout the coming week, use this prayer as part of your conversation with God.

Chapter Thirteen
Sometimes My Life Feels Like a Cliffhanger

FIND

He shall cover you with His feathers,
And under His wings you shall take refuge;
His truth shall be your shield and buckler.
You shall not be afraid of the terror by night,
Nor the arrow that flies by day. (Psalm 91:4-5)

1. Read the passage above. Why do you sometimes find it hard to trust God?
2. Read Proverbs 3:5-6. List some of the things or people you have trusted in the past. How did your trust of these things or people affect your relationship with God?
3. How do you know you can trust God?

FEEL

1. How does it make you feel to trust someone? Are you anxious, scared, relieved? Explain your response.
2. We are told in Scripture that trying to figure out everything ourselves and trusting God are mutually exclusive. Think about the past month or so. Which have you done more—tried to figure out things for yourself or trusted God? How would your closest friend answer that question about you?
3. Describe a time when you have felt angry at or distrusting of God. What caused you to have those feelings?

FOLLOW

1. List a few of the speed bumps in your life. How has each affected your spiritual vitality?
2. As you have drawn closer to God, what has He changed about you?
3. Think about those things you fear most. Write your fears in the space below and then search for Bible passages that address those fears. Write the passage next to each fear and begin committing those passages to memory.
4. How does your attitude toward trusting others affect your willingness to trust God?

5. What could be a first step for you in trusting God no matter how small it may seem?
6. Write a prayer expressing your desires. Throughout the coming week, use this prayer as part of your conversation with God.

Chapter Fourteen
God Will Prove It's a Love Story

FIND

For God so loved the world that He gave His only begotten Son, that whoever believes in Him should not perish but have everlasting life. For God did not send his Son into the world to condemn the world, but that the world through Him might be saved. (John 3:16-17)

1. You have read or heard the passage above many times. Rewrite the passage replacing "the world" and "whoever" with your name.
2. Read your personalized version of John 3:16-17. Why would God love you this much?
3. Describe a time when you have replaced your trust in God with trust in someone or something else. What was the outcome of that situation?

FEEL

1. You are the object of God's greatest love story. How does that make you feel?
2. One of the greatest gifts God gave you is the ability to communicate with Him without delay or fear. Describe the quality of your conversations with God. What do you most often talk about?

3. How does God most often speak to you? How do you know it's God?
4. Read Psalm 98:6. How does the truth of that verse make you feel?

FOLLOW

1. God wants you to hear His voice worse than you want to hear it. What are some of the distractions that keep you from hearing Him?
2. God provided everything Adam and Eve needed. In what areas of your life do you need God to provide?
3. In what areas of life do you need to let go of a wrong understanding of the love of God?
4. Write a prayer expressing your desires. Throughout the coming week, use this prayer as part of your conversation with God.

Chapter Fifteen
We Are What We Believe We Are?

FIND

And the Lord *God said, "It is not good that man should be alone; I will make him a helper comparable to him."* (Genesis. 2:18)

1. Describe yourself from God's perspective.
2. What are the things about you that bother God most?
3. Describe a time when you have chosen to bring your will in line with God's truth and walk away from negative thoughts about yourself.

FEEL

1. If you are disappointed in yourself, you assume God is too. How do you feel when you think God is disappointed in you?
2. Reflect on a time in your life when you felt really good about yourself. What led to that feeling?
3. Read John 8:3-11. How would you have felt had you been in the woman's situation? How would you have felt once you were forgiven by Jesus?

FOLLOW

1. Take a piece of paper and write down all of the negative things you can remember from as far back as possible. Then, ask God to remove those negatives and to let you see yourself from His perspective.
2. What are some things you have believed about God that might not be true?
3. What small secrets are you hiding?
4. What do you want God to do in and through your life in the days and weeks ahead?
5. Write a prayer expressing your desires. Throughout the coming week, use this prayer as part of your conversation with God.

Chapter Sixteen
Table for Two, Please

FIND

Love never gives up.
Love cares more for others than for self.
Love doesn't want what it doesn't have.

Love doesn't strut,
Doesn't have a swelled head,
Doesn't force itself on others,
Isn't always "me first,"
Doesn't fly off the handle,
Doesn't keep score of the sins of others,
Doesn't revel when others grovel,
Takes pleasure in the flowering of truth,
Puts up with anything,
Trusts God always,
Always looks for the best,
Never looks back,
But keeps going to the end. (1 Corinthians 13:4-7 MSG)

1. Read the passage above and place a check mark by the phrases that are easy for you. Why is it difficult to consistently express love the way the Bible describes it?
2. Describe how God's love has radically transformed your life.
3. Read Luke 19:10. Jesus came to restore you from your brokenness. From what hurts do you need God's restoration?
4. Jesus came looking for Zacchaeus. For whom in your life is Jesus looking, and what might be your role in showing that person God's love?

FEEL

1. Jesus came looking for you. How does that fact make you feel?
2. If Jesus came looking for you, what would make Him turn His back on you?

3. Because Jesus loves you, you can begin each day with purpose and peace. Reflect on the past few days and describe the peace you have experienced. What interrupted your peace? What brought you more peace?

FOLLOW

1. Describe a time when you lost something important. How did you feel?
2. Who is someone in your life who seems too far away for God to reach?
3. Reflect on the fact that the very cells of your body that hold you together are in the shape of a cross, and let the wonder fill you up. Write a prayer expressing your desires. Throughout the coming week, use this prayer as part of your conversation with God.

Chapter Seventeen
No Light at the End of My Tunnel

FIND

Alongside Babylon's rivers we sat on the banks; we cried and cried,
remembering the good old days in Zion.
Alongside the quaking aspens
we stacked our unplayed harps;
That's where our captors demanded songs,
sarcastic and mocking:
"Sing us a happy Zion song!"
Oh, how could we ever sing God's song
in this wasteland? (Psalm 137:1-4 MSG)

1. Maybe you've felt like you've been in a wasteland with no light at the end of life's tunnel. What do you know about God that gives you hope?
2. Who are some friends who can support you in your search for hope and restoration?
3. Reflect on a time when Satan made you think a lie was the truth. How did you discover the truth?

FEEL

1. God promises to deliver you from whatever struggle you are facing. He also promises to sustain you through life's struggles. How can you make these facts more real in your life?
2. God is telling you three things. Complete each statement.
    - Because God wants me to let go of trying to fix this, I will . . .
    - Because God wants me to let go of trying to work out what will happen, I will . . .
    - Because God wants me to let go of trying to protect myself, I will . . .

   How do you feel after completing each statement?

FOLLOW

1. Satan would love to convince you right now that there is no hope in your situation. What will be your response to Satan's accusations?
2. Hope is your resting place because you put your trust in Jesus Christ. How can you strengthen your dependence on Jesus to see you through your life experiences?

3. What do you believe God is asking you to let go?
4. Write a prayer expressing your desires. Throughout the coming week, use this prayer as part of your conversation with God.

Chapter Eighteen
The Million-Watt Megabulb of God's Hope

FIND

Through thick and thin, keep your hearts at attention, in adoration before Christ, your Master. Be ready to speak up and tell anyone who asks why you're living the way you are, and always with the utmost courtesy. (1 Peter 3:15 MSG)

1. Read the verse above and make a list of some things you can do to be ready to speak up and share what God is doing in your life.
2. How does God reveal hope to you?
3. Read Psalm 66:1-4. What is God saying to you through this passage?
4. In what have you place your hope in the past? Why was that an unwise choice?

FEEL

1. Describe some things you have done to build your hope on Christ. Why were these things effective hope-builders?
2. How do you feel today in comparison to how you felt when the study began?
3. What have been some of the most helpful lessons you have learned?

FOLLOW

1. Read Matthew 7:24-26. How would you describe your spiritual foundation today? What can you do to make it stronger? Against what negative influences do you need to guard yourself?
2. How would you define hope today?
3. In what areas of life do you still need a more solid foundation?
4. How can you intentionally take every thought captive?
5. Write a prayer expressing your desires for yourself and your family. Throughout the coming week, use this prayer as part of your conversation with God.

ABOUT THE AUTHOR

Sheila Walsh is a powerful communicator, Bible teacher, and best-selling author with more than 4 million books sold. A featured speaker with Women of Faith, Sheila has reached more than 3.5 million women by artistically combining honesty, vulnerability, and humor with God's Word.

Author of the best-selling memoir *Honestly* and the Gold Medallion nominee for *The Heartache No One Sees*, Sheila's most recent releases, *The Shelter of God's Promises* and *Beautiful Things Happen When A Woman Trusts God*, include a 12-week Bible study. The *Gigi, God's Little Princess* book and video series has won the National Retailer's Choice Award twice and is the most popular Christian brand for young girls in the United States.

Sheila co-hosted *The 700 Club* and her own show *Heart to Heart with Sheila Walsh*. She is currently completing her Masters in Theology and lives in Dallas, Texas, with her husband, Barry, son, Christian, and two little dogs.